*Edgar Morin*

## Modern European Thinkers Series

Series Editor: Professor Keith Reader,
University of Newcastle upon Tyne

The Modern European Thinkers series offers low-priced introductions for students and other readers to the ideas and work of key cultural and political thinkers of the post-war era.

For a complete list of available titles please contact the Pluto Press office.

Régis Debray: A Critical Introduction
*Keith Reader*

Guy Hocquenghem
*Bill Marshall*

Fraternité.

A Paris, chez Basset, rue Jacques, au coin de celle des Mathurins.

# Edgar Morin

## From Big Brother to Fraternity

*Myron Kofman*

LONDON • CHICAGO, IL.

First published 1996 by Pluto Press
345 Archway Road, London N6 5AA
and 1436 West Randolph,
Chicago, Illinois 60607, USA



British Library Cataloguing in Publication Data
A catalogue record for this book is available from the British Library

ISBN 0 7453 0851 1 hbk

Library of Congress Cataloging in Publication Data available

Printing history 99 98 97 96 5 4 3 2 1

Designed and produced for Pluto Press by
Chase Production Services, Chipping Norton, OX7 5QR
Typeset from disk by Stanford DTP Services, Milton Keynes
Printed in the EC by The Cromwell Press,
Broughton Gifford, England

# Contents

# Acknowledgements

I have a large moral debt to David Bell of Leeds University, Mike Fuller and Malcolm Pittock of Bolton Institute who each discussed the manuscript with me, to Roger Chapman who discussed chapter 6 and to Sharon Higgins who produced the manuscript.

The frontispiece illustration, Fraternité, is reproduced with permission from Phototheque des Musées de la Ville de Paris, by SPADEM.

# Preface

The career of Edgar Morin is bound up with the utopian Marxism of the post-Second World War French intellectuals and the subsequent search for the new directions when the hopes of the age of Marxism collapsed. Morin is today a saviour of a world without salvation. Born 1921, Morin joined the Communist Party in 1942 and left it in 1951. His *Autocritique* of 1959 became the classic autobiography of a journey to the end of 'the Party'; it started Morin on his path in which interrogation of the world and interrogation of self would be connected as an intellectual strategy.

Morin was marginal in 1960s' France: if we consider Morin's way as a revival of Montaigne's scepticism after three centuries when it was subdued by cartesian certainties we can appreciate why in the 1960s, last decade of ideological faiths, he went against the grain. The structuralist determinism of an Althusser or Lacan gave no value to Morin's incessant self-questioning. In the 1970s Morin's intellectual development caught the eruption of a crisis in the French, if not European, intellectual community. *La Méthode*, his major work, is post-Marx and post-Descartes. Out of the cosmic tissue of paradoxes and indeterminism engendered by twentieth-century physics Morin wove a method committed to the ever-growing complexity of philosophy and the human and natural sciences. Their unity is no longer produced by a determinist schema but is a work of self-organisation in which the sciences are connected but remain autonomous.

Morin's approach is in harmony with a new culture of uncertainty as instanced in the literary and philosophic writings of Derrida, Levinas or Deleuze. But unlike his fellow travellers Morin has been alone in daring to attempt a method which connects sciences and philosophy through complexity. In French intellectual life today Morin is now a leader but still an outsider.

# Chronology

| | |
|---|---|
| 1921 | Born of Sephardic parents Vidal and Luna Nahum |
| 1930 | Luna dies |
| 1938 | Joins the anarcho-syndicalist journal, *La Flèche* |
| 1940 | German invasion; escapes to Vichy |
| 1942 | Joins Communists – underground name Morin |
| 1944 | Liberation: Morin leading young communist intellectual; first political 'euphoria' |
| 1949 | Ceases active membership |
| 1950 | Joins CNRS |
| 1951 | Expelled from PCF |
| 1956 | Khrushchev denounces Stalin; Soviet invasion of Hungary; Morin founds *Arguments* |
| 1959 | Algerian uprising; Morin avoids commitment |
| 1962 | *Arguments* dissolved; Morin hospitalised |
| 1968 (May) | Student 'revolution'; Morin's cool enthusiasm |
| 1969–70 | Research year in California; disengages from French politics |
| 1970–74 | Organises international colloquium on 'unity of man' |
| 1975 | Denounces Portuguese Left's threat to press freedom |
| 1989–91 | Collapse of Soviet communism; Morin's last 'euphoria' |
| 1977–91 | Publishes the four volumes of *La Méthode* |

CHAPTER 1

# Morin's Ark

In the 1980s Edgar Morin became recognised in France as one of the grand old men of French letters and a major figure in European intellectual life. In 1994 he was consecrated 'Morin'.[1] (To be published under surname alone is an ultimate accolade of fame.) His range is encylopedic: his works occupy bookshop shelves in philosophy, the natural sciences, sociology as well as in sections on the Soviet Union, Europe and French politics. *La Méthode*, his major work, is itself an encyclopedia in the scope of intellectual territory it occupies.

Morin's publications in his own classification are listed on pages 123–5. In chronological terms they cover nearly half a century, beginning in 1946. Morin classifies them over and across traditional disciplinary boundaries. Thus much of *La Méthode* and *Complex Thought* could normally be classified under philosophy; that *Sociologie* is included under *Complex Thought* rather than human sciences (*anthropologie fondamentale*) alerts us to his desire to undermine conventions about what constitutes a discipline. That Morin assigns his two books on film, *Le cinéma* and *Les stars*, to human sciences and twentieth century respectively suggests the importance he gives to context.

*Twentieth Century*, the largest group, includes works of commentary on events and processes from French politics, society, Europe, communism as well as film. Morin writes not only as observer of social and political events; in several works Morin was also participant and even catalyst in the processes he described. If in May 1968 he was part observer, part participant, in *Report from a French Village* he was participant and catalyst: in this example of interventionist sociology the investigator deliberately enters into the society he investigates.

The works of commentary predominate before 1970 while the more theoretical writings predominate afterwards. The structure of this work connects this chronological shift to an intellectual, possibly emotional, conversion Morin experienced in California in 1969.

Reference to conversion introduces a striking feature of Morin's list, namely the large number of autobiographies. Indeed Morin's reference to his own life is even more pervasive than his classification shows, since it occurs in most works. Morin may be the most self-referential thinker in French since Montaigne. His hostility to the notion of rigid, objective boundaries between disciplines owes much to his insistence on the primacy of personal experience.

Connected to the strong imprint of Morin's personality he is seen as the voice, if not prophet, of a new humanism and a renovation of thinking. The extent to which this dimension is felt outside of France is marked by the range of translations and symposiums devoted to him as well as by the syndication of his articles in Italy, Spain, South and North America as well as the Far East. And yet this is the first English book to address his life and thought; the contrast cannot be explained only by the principle that intellectual goods, especially outside the natural sciences, are severely damaged in translation. The asymmetry (between Britain and much of the world) presents a challenge and an opportunity.

### *Morin's Place in European Thought*

Morin's significance is to have been the most far-ranging thinker of the concept (or paradigm) of self-organisation. This concept in Morin's development connects but does not unify physics, biology, the human sciences and philosophy in what he sees as a grand and good circular motion. In this enterprise he has many counterparts on the American continent such as Gregory Bateson, Francisco Varela and Maryuama, and several allies in France of whom the most crucial to his enterprise are Prigogine and Stengers, and Henri Atlan (although Atlan commutes between the Seine and Jerusalem).[2] At their core are the works of Ilia Prigogine and Isabel Stengers which extend an indeterminist approach to the problems of physics they share with Popper into a metaphysics of the 'Arrow of Time'. Instead of causal mechanisms happening within time they argue for processes of the degradation and of the creation of order as essential to time itself. Morin gives this resulting concept of self-organisation (as going deeper than causality) its widest possible employment beyond its origin in physics so as to engender a loop between human society and the physical universe. Such a vision implies a reconciliation of science and myth termed 'mythico-real' by Morin; the expression can alert us to a superficial resemblance between Morin and Michel Serres, who has interpreted scientific theories as myths, but the concept of mythico-real interdicts the reduction of science to myth.[3]

The distinctive expansiveness, ambition (and mysticism) in Morin's enterprise derives from the way he recast the Hegelian Marxism with which he operated until 1970. I present him as the most utopian of Hegelian Marxists (chapters 3 and 4) before he became the most Hegelian of theorists of self-organisation. He did not abandon dialectical thought but expanded it into what he termed the paradigm of complexity (also complex thought) of which the principal strand is the dialogic. The word was coined by Bakhtin in Soviet Russia *circa* 1929. Morin created his concept without knowing Bakhtin, although Bakhtin's concept of polyvocal, non-hierarchic culture will be seen to foreshadow Morin's concept of multiplicity of logics. Whether Morin's usage successfully challenges Bakhtin's could eventually prove a litmus test of his place in intellectual history. (Bakhtin's has been adopted by Kristeva.)

The force which drove Morin's rethinking was an insistence he shared with all the thinkers of 'self-organisation' that the sciences in the late twentieth century had reached a crisis of meaning comparable to that which resulted in Newtonian physics and the determinism of the Enlightenment. This crisis was particularly evident in physics but allegedly affected even the apparent victories of the old determinism when they occurred – as in molecular biology. In all cases coherence seemed lost as scientific explanation ran into paradoxes, circularities and contradictions. Self-organisation is a paradigm in that it does not solve the difficulties of the crisis, but is a *guide* to clearing a path through its entanglements. But the background of dialectical thought was crucial in Morin's very specific response. Although dialectic offered to overcome the limitations of formal logic, after 1970 Morin would come to characterise the path of the dialectic as a 'reassuring rationalisation'. Thus the paradigm of complexity, quite distinct from mere complication and in contrast to dialectical thought, would live with paradox and contradiction. Now it is this dialectic path by which Morin arrived at the paradigm of complexity that led him to adopt the concept of the dialogic; moreover this path gave his work a cultural and political drive charged with messianic significance in the context of postwar French intellectual history. For in Morin's perspective the crisis of science was part of a more general catastrophe in which Marxism was unavoidably engulfed and which he saw accomplished in France in the 1970s, indeed essentially between 1973 and 1975.

### *Recognition as Master Thinker*

Such a vision of catastrophe is apocalyptic; because Morin believed that the paradigm of complexity is a promise of rescue, it is also messianic ... and he himself becomes a reluctant messiah. It is this cultural-political dimension, inseparable from Morin's intellectual inventiveness (and his weaknesses) that I have sought to express in the subtitle to this work.

No English-speaking reader needs to be introduced to Big Brother. For Morin Big Brother was not only Stalin or the French

Communist Party (PCF) but (*after* 1970) Marxism. The word 'fraternity' is for Morin the conceptual vehicle for the self-organisation of life and living societies but it is also an element of the fundamental self-valuation of the French republican state. I shall argue that Morin effectively connects the two senses of fraternity in the union he terms 'mythico-real'. Thus the process whereby Morin was accepted as a master thinker was one where his own development came to the rescue of the 'intelligentsia de gauche' which, having marginalised Morin before 1975, now needed him in its time of trouble.

The recognition Morin achieved in the 1980s was based on a major intellectual achievement in the political culture of France. The apocalyptic-messianic sense of Morin's work encountered the cultural catastrophe of Marxism precisely in the years he was elaborating the paradigm of complexity.[4]

In this context his message of a 'politics of man' could capitalise on the intimations of scepticism and uncertainty which affected not only the French but much of the international intellectual community. Moreover, in this real catastrophe Morin's reworking of Hegel would give him an evolutionary advantage. My exposition will emphasise that Morin the Hegelian Marxist had already been engaged in mapping the connection between philosophy and science and that he had been particularly adventurous in exploring the prospect of using science in the satisfaction of human needs.

After 1970 Morin's perception of the sciences would centre on their crisis of meaning rather than their promise of fulfilment. But to this new vision he brought an equally exalted enthusiasm. Thus Morin could agree with many of the negative, 'deconstructionist' approaches of Jacques Derrida, but he could offer this vision not only with the accent but with the method of hope. To indicate that he not only saw himself but could be seen by others as the saviour of a world without salvation I propose to term the combination of Morin and his enterprise 'Morin's Ark'.

### *Barriers against Morin in Anglo-American Culture*

Morin's role as saviour from the catastrophe of Marxism will go some way to indicating the difficulty his work had in crossing over to one English-speaking world. The decision to finish with his Marxist past because Marxism was finished came to Morin after 1970; we need only remember that the 1970s were the golden years of Marxist theory in Anglo-American culture (when Morin's bugbear Althusser became a household name in the socialist community) to see one dimension of the barrier before Morin's work in Britain and in the USA.

This barrier could even operate retrospectively, that is, it could diminish the perceived significance of Morin the Hegelian Marxist. An illustration is the minuscule place Morin occupied in Mark Poster's American Marxist history *Existentialist Marxism in Post-war France*, where his role as creator and inspirer of the journal *Arguments* is imperfectly visible.[5]

But the other crucial barrier is Morin's comprehensive use of complex thought as a way of connecting 'the sciences'. It gave Morin's uniquely broad version of the self-organisation approach the aspect of a crusade against a French ruling orthodoxy of 'les sciences' when that orthodoxy either did not hold in mainstream English philosophy of science or held in a way which was almost invisible to its proponents.[6]

The polemical antagonist of Morin's crusade was concentrated in structuralist determinism. This 'reigning orthodoxy' held that all scientific knowledge is subject to (determined by) an invariant set of laws. Each science is understood as a specific field of knowledge with a structure such that it is conceptually immune to other sciences.

A wide range of spatial metaphors were used to affirm the existence of a conceptual immune system or intransitivity between the sciences. Each science was expected to set up for itself a unique object or field; one metaphor particularly derided by Morin is that of the separate continents of physics, biology and the human sciences. Sometimes even individual human sciences were seen as continents, as when Althusser declared that Marx had set up the 'continent' of history.[7]

In opposition to this orthodoxy Morin declared for the opening of frontiers between the sciences; a favourite metaphor is that of the poacher smuggling illicit and yet conceptually essential intellectual goods from one discipline to another. A central instance to be analysed in chapter 5 is Morin's enjoyment of the 'contraband' aspects of the words 'programme' and 'code' when they were imported into molecular biology from linguistics and cybernetics.

Now English intellectual life has been predominantly concerned with the nature of the laws of science. The issue of theorising the relationship between scientific disciplines has not generated the same polemical and ideological heat as in France. Evidence of this divergence exists in the language of characterising 'les sciences', or rather in English understatement of the terminology of 'the sciences' (an unusual expression in English). Certainly the practice of isolating the 'sciences' as non-communicating domains occurs in English as in French academic discipline. But the fervour of Morin's crusade against frontiers and customs barriers together with his glorification of intellectual poaching, loses most of its colour in the English cultural atmosphere without necessarily losing any of its intellectual thrust. In the English context Morin's project of connecting the sciences through the method of self-organisation is still in radical opposition to a philosophy of science in which all science can be united under a single law or set of laws. It is still in marked contrast to an academic life which *in practice* divides the lawfulness of things into discrete disciplines. But since these divisions are not buttressed by theories which regard the establishment of frontier posts as a fundamental requirement of 'a science' the polemical thrust of Morin's insistence on transdisciplinarity is blunted.

Having presented Morin as a thinker whose radicalism had a polemical thrust specific to French intellectual life we can now return to the question of Morin's 'recognition' as a master thinker. To be recognised in this context records legitimation or acceptance by the intellectual community, the community itself being self-appointed. In its specifically French context this problem has at its core Morin's place among 'Les intellectuels'. Such placing (which can never be precise or static) can be sought by criteria of achievement but also in terms of cultural, ideological and institutional contexts,[8] which do not only decide the perceived value of a body of work but place it as central, marginal or eccentric in a given culture. My reference to the 'consecration' of Morin indicates that he has now found ultimate acceptance in France. This acceptance is counterpointed by Morin's own perception of himself as an outsider: marginal if not eccentric. Such discrepancy is a recurring aspect of the debate on intellectual power, fuelled as it is by self-dramatisation. It is ironic that the word consecration was popularised by Morin's 'worst enemy', the ultra-determinist sociologist Pierre Bourdieu, who, we can note, persistently misrepresented himself as an outsider.[9] The story of Morin will in fact help expose the futility of a narrowly sociological approach to consecration. Morin will be shown to have been an outsider who became a 'master thinker' thanks to a cultural revolution in which he participated; nevertheless Morin remains an outsider. Morin's own neologism 'mythico-real' well fits the shifting character of 'le pouvoir intellectuel'.

I propose to structure my analysis in this chapter as follows. The first section will present Morin's achievement as a biography; it will touch on the great ideological revolution of Morin's adulthood – the collapse of Marxism-Leninism as the dominant intellectual power in France. This happened in the 1970s, earlier than elsewhere in the West, and came with catastrophic speed.

The next section will divide in two parts: the first will present Morin's own account of the ecological catastrophe; the second will use Morin's account to explain why Morin could establish for himself a quasi messianic persona.

## *Morin's Biography*

Morin was born in 1921.[10] His father, Vidal Nahum, a Sephardic Jew, came from Salonica, a vestige of the Greco-Roman polyglot, cosmopolitan world city. His mother, Luna, died when he was nine. Later he discovered that she had tried to abort believing the foetus endangered her life; the labour nearly killed her and he survived strangulation by the umbilical cord.[11] Morin's father's legacy was *diaspora* and cosmopolitanism, the world as dispersion and home, his mother's was the thin line between life and death. Their combined legacy was one of loss. The loss of Luna was real, of Vidal symbolic when, in the Resistance, Edgar Nahum took the French surname Morin, his 'fraternity' name.[12] When Vidal died in 1984 Morin published an article as Morin-Nahum, so partially restoring his father's name. Finally 'Morin' fully asserted his Sephardic roots in his family history *Vidal*.

Morin's introduction to politics came in the Paris of the 1930s with its squalls of revolutionary expectancy and their depressed subsidence. The Popular Front of 1935–6 had promised revolution by uniting the Left; by 1938 it had collapsed.[13] Morin's horizons of fraternity, revolution and youthful dreams consequently shrank. He associated with *La Flèche*, a journal trapped between socialism, anarchism and pacifism. The trap was inherent in the hopelessness of 1930s' pacifism. It was a prayer that the great dictators leave France alone. Hitler's invasion turned the cultivated French garden into a 'tohu-bohu' (chaos). Morin escaped to Toulouse in the partial safety of Vichy France. The courses he had followed at the Sorbonne were interrupted; he would not complete a degree; the war made him both academic and autodidact.

Until the Reichswehr failed to take Moscow late in 1941 Morin was convinced the Third Reich represented a new European order. Only the Soviet victory at Stalingrad made hope certain. Late in 1942, coupling the exhilaration and awe produced by Soviet power, Morin joined the PCF; he left it in 1951.

His encounter with 'apparatus communism' as a system inducing a sense of trial and guilt was the great trauma of his life. In 1959 he would articulate and dramatise the experience in *Autocritique*, an intellectual 'bestseller' and a key to the phenomenon of existential Marxism, as will be seen in chapter 2.

Between 1951 and 1956 Morin was in political purdah as an ex-communist – an untouchable on the French Left. The dominant ideology of commitment meant that non-communists not only admired the PCF but regarded anyone who left it as a renegade. (The most notorious example came in 1956 when Sartre denounced Pierre Hervé, expelled from the PCF for criticising its sectarianism.) In career terms a new life began in 1950: he was recruited by Georges Friedmann, foremost sociologist of the non-Marxist Left, to the *Centre National de la Récherche Scientifique* (CNRS). Founded before the war, CNRS, with encouragement from the French state, became a major centre of research; it was promoted as a counterweight to the traditional humanities-oriented university system and the *Hautes Écoles,* rigidly organised around the traditional disciplines. It was, for Morin, an ideal intellectual space almost in the sense that Versailles was Louis XIV's ideal theatrical space ('almost', since Morin did not create CNRS). He was soon among Friedman's principal collaborators in the section CECMAS (Centre d'Études de Communications de Masse) which in 1972 Morin renamed as a centre of transdisciplinary studies (Sociology, Anthropology, Semiology), headed initially by a triumvirate, Friedmann, Morin and Barthes, already at the height of fame for his readings of signs in culture, before Morin assumed its presidency in 1978.[14] The institution was an instrument which Morin could shape into a vehicle of transdisciplinarity, not only a counterweight, but a challenge to the traditional system.

Morin's first political step when he emerged from his shadow world came in 1957, the year he founded *Arguments*, a journal intended to function as a forum of open Marxism and undogmatic debate.

In 1962 *Arguments* was closed down. Despite its financial viability, its 'captains', Morin, Kostas Axelos and Jean Duvignaud decided to scuttle it. They explained the decision as a search for new horizons. As the years went by Morin was to recognise the real significance of this 'gentle suicide'.[15] It took place in the year when the hope of a Marxism open equally to Sartre as to Khrushchev was finally extinguished. Moreover, unknown to Morin, a new star, Althusser, began to shine over Marxism. (Althusser's articles in communist journals began to attract attention just as *Arguments* folded.)

It was also a year of personal crisis for Morin:[16] it mirrored and transformed the ideological watershed marked by the suicide of *Arguments*. His first marriage, a tie which had begun in Toulouse at the high tide of the Resistance, broke down. While visiting America he suffered a heart disorder and was hospitalised, at the Mount Sinai Clinic. These breakdowns seem to mirror the end of the Resistance–existentialist era of the Parisian intelligentsia; while recovering in hospital Morin decided to plunge deeper in the search for a method to connect the human sciences, physics and biology. Morin himself saw the illness as a sign that his previous mode of life was at a dead end.

The end of *Arguments* was an element in the regroupings which articulated the breakdown of the existential Marxist paradigm of

1944–62 (the paradigm itself will be analysed in the following section). I distinguish between Morin's ideological repositioning and the thrust of his conceptual reconsiderations. Ideologically Morin, former captain of *Arguments*, joined forces with Castoriadis and Lefort from *Socialisme ou barbarie* (henceforth *SB*), who, like Morin, had also scuttled their journal.[17] *SB* was the forum of 'anarcho-Marxist' theory. Its contributors began as Trotskyist dissidents and elaborated an approach which based socialist revolution on workers' control. The often remarked contrast between the 'gentle suicide' of *Arguments* and the violent implosion of *SB* is indicative of Morin's personal and intellectual priorities. Castoriadis (who wrote much of *SB* under three pseudonyms: Paul Cardan, Pierre Chaulieu, Jean-Yves Delvaux) had broken with Marxism seeing it as inadequate for revolutionary socialism; he sought an alternative socio-economic theory to drive revolutionary activism, an arena Morin was leaving. Thus the alliance fully functioned only once and that occasion was May 1968, a world turned upside down. Their joint production, *Mai '68* celebrated the unification of Marx, anarchy and revolution as creative energy. Morin's contribution, which exalted its youth, subsequently read as a farewell.

Morin's intellectual priorities were shifting: in 1966 he became a founder member of an interdisciplinary club of researchers, the 'group of ten' including Henri Laborit, the biologist, and Jacques Sauvan, the cyberneticist. He imprinted his appetite for dissolving specialist concerns on the group. His quests discouraged the political alignment with the socialists which some members desired.[18]

In 1969 Morin went to California with two agendas. Alongside his official posting with the Salk Institute for Biological Research was a pilgrimage to the birthplace of youth culture. Now came the event which Morin saw as the revelation he had been seeking ever since he was hospitalised. His appetite for the scientific revolution proved deeper than for the cultural revolution: when he returned to Paris the sense of vocation for a project to create a meta-concept of the sciences was palpable to his colleagues. He dedicated *Californie* to Salk and to Jacques Monod.

Monod's *Le Hasard et la Nécessité* changed Morin. He discerned in it an interplay of order and disorder. Since Monod claimed his work had evacuated dialectics from biology, Morin was enlisting Monod against Monod.

Morin's appropriation of Monod exemplified the boldness of an autodidact, a measured willingness to transgress which enhanced his intellectual and institutional influence. His unorthodox use of many specialists did not significantly lose him an audience in the specialist 'university' establishment but did attract much interest from groups on the outskirts of mainstream science and philosophy, especially Catholics from *Oméga*, followers of Teilhard de Chardin.[19]

Morin thus touched, without adopting, teleological or holistic philosophies of science. Both in molecular biology and in cybernetics the specialists Morin 'interrogated' invoked teleonomy, that is, models of purposive system without the recourse to an ultimate purpose or purposer of the traditional concept of teleology. I shall explore Morin's concept of organisation as self-generating systems in chapter 6. But we can preliminarily place this concept as a radical expansion of approaches in a second wave of systems theory. Indeed, certain passages in *La Méthode*, read 'literally', seem to cross the divide into the mystical visions of Teilhard de Chardin or, more modestly, into the attempts of David Bohm to establish theoretically the physical oneness of the universe, transcending space time, under the rubric of 'implicate order'.[20] Morin, however, distanced himself from teleological holism in two apparently divergent ways:

- He explicitly placed his method under the sign of a universe without purpose or purposer (teleonomy).
- He emphasised the 'tragic' role of disorder in the universe to the point of inviting the rebuke that disorder and tragedy had become a mystique in his hands.[21]

Later I argue that these two prongs reconnect, that Morin developed a theory which allows the existence of a transcendental unity but is ever anxious to ensure that the mystical force cannot turn out to be a disguise of power, namely of Big Brother. Here, however, my concern is to indicate the ideological and institutional context which Morin's mystical scepticism generated for him.

Morin's intellectual persona was that of a 'marginal' struggling to liberate thought from the dominant orthodoxies of reductionism, determinism, simplification and specialisation. In the 1970s he would unhesitatingly identify his enemy number one as the dominance of structuralist Marxism but more generally of Marxisms in France. The ideological shift connected with a crisis of identity which Morin experienced as cultural and emotional: in the aftermath of the 1973 petrol crisis he discovered an affection for Europe as a vulnerable mother which would curb his celebration of energy whirlpools such as California or May 1968.[22] Together with his international and intercontinental commitments Europeanism further distanced him from the specificities of French politics.

Increasingly, after 1970, Morin organised around himself a society of investigators or thinkers who would work outside specifically political concerns. My reference to Morin's entry into CNRS already touched on the opportunity it provided for his talents as a one-man ginger group *within* an institutional framework.

On his return from California, Morin created CIEFAB (Centre Internationale d'Études Bioanthropiques et d'Anthropologie Fondamentale). This became the 'centre Royaumont pour une science de L'Homme'. He then organised an international colloquium on 'L'Unité de l'homme' in 1972, in collaboration with Massimo Piatelli-Palmarini. The proceedings, published in three volumes, provided a setting of interrogation with some leading names in biology, cybernetics and the human sciences on the European and American continent: Atlan, Monod, Jacob, Von Foerster, Maturana, Moscovoci, Le Roy Ladurie and Premack. Monod would be the first president of Royaumont, Morin the second (1976–8).[23]

As a corollary Morin himself became an international personage with a particularly strong following in the Italian, Spanish and Portuguese speaking worlds. Portugal would provide the one instance of a political intervention in the 1970s when Morin published articles defending freedom of the press against threats emanating from a communist-led Left in 1975.[24] Such direct activism was an exception which illuminated the rule. Despite Morin's eminence among the writers who argued for the irreducibly totalitarian nature of the Soviet system he would stay politically aloof: in the decisive ideological struggle to defend Solidarnosc against communist pressure in Poland he was only a supporter of initiatives which came from Castoriadis and Alain Touraine. Morin's public voice would be that of a new humanism aloof not only from the decay of Marxism but from the ancient mythologies of socialism.

## *Farewell to Marxism*

In Morin's own story of the rise and fall of French Marxism he inevitably appeared in the script. He wrote two major versions, one in *Twentieth Century* when the end was in sight, the other, 'That which has changed in French intellectual life' in 1986 when the great 'ecological catastrophe' was completed. Morin's presuppositions, lacunas and self-references indicate why the persona of a saviour in a world bereft of salvation should find a major audience in France.

Morin's analysis is profoundly subjective; its perspective on intellectual history is that of the 'intelligentsia de gauche', of which Morin himself is a member.[25] The term *intelligentsia*, the Russian for 'intellectual', expresses a prescriptive vision of 'l'intellectuel', namely as a creative and critical spirit.

Echoing and expanding Sartre's famous distinction between the intellectual and the expert (an atomic physicist is an expert but if he signs an anti-nuclear manifesto he becomes an intellectual), Morin characterised the activity of the intellectual as:

- the production of myths and ideologies working in culture, society and politics;
- The critique of myths and ideologies.[26]

This definition will lead back to Morin.

### *The Ages of Marxism*

Morin dated Marxist hegemony in France from 1945 to 1973–5. He closed it with an image of profound desolation: 'deprived of its mythological source of youthfulness the sublime doctrine, like she who must be obeyed, fell to ashes'.[27] In the film of Rider Haggard's novel, *She* (Ursula Andress) is transformed into a pile of 2000-year-old ashes: comparing Marxism to *She* makes the verdict blacker than black.

And yet in the beginning Morin saw promise: 1945–57, the first phase, was marked by a combination of 'philosophic defrosting and ideological frost'. But the philosophic discoveries – Hegel, Husserl, existentialism, and the Hegelian Marxism of Lukacs – were captured by the ideological corset of a Marxism acceptable to the communists.

In 1957 came a thaw on the back of Khrushchev's de-Stalinisation and of the Hungarian uprising. *Arguments* was the journal of this spring: it offered the Left a multi-dimensional Marxism and interrogative thinking. So, for Morin, the demise of *Arguments* implicitly marked the end of the road for French Marxism. In 1962 a new frost arrived: not one theory but a 'minestrone' of structuralism and epistemologism in which knowledge represented only the conventions of an ideology. They were united by claims to absolute scientificity whether the claimants were formal Marxists (Althusser) or not (Lévi Strauss, Lacan, Foucault). Their alliance combined to make History unproblematic and killed off the problem of subjectivity. The determinisms of structural linguistics modelled myth, the unconscious, society. Knowledge was to be rigidly determined by Foucault, as the episteme (mind set) of any given epoch.[28] (In contrast to the paradigm of complexity which is a guide not a straightjacket.)

This ice age hit its trough *circa* 1966–7 when the Gaullist modernisation of France seemed most secure. It drew its energy from distant Marxist suns shining from China, Vietnam or Cuba.

For Morin, French Marxism had become brain dead, kept alive by external inputs, although the 'whirlwind' of May 1968 gave it the spurious appearance of having received new energy: 'A counter culture nourishing the values of desire ... as well as the myth of the revolutionary Apocalypse.'[29]

But the emptiness of 'epistemo-structuralism' transpired from the meagre harvest it garnered from the values of desire – the one valid input of May 1968. The epistemo-structuralist corset deformed desire into Gilles Deleuze's concept of humans as 'desiring machines'

In 1973, according to Morin, 'She' began her collapse as the distant red suns all imploded. The events Morin instanced all occurred outside France, so reinforcing the image of a clinically dead being whose life support was finally cut off. Mao and China, so near in 1968, vanished ideologically between 1971 and 1976, the People's Vietnam of 1975 became colonialist and oppressive, Cambodia a mad concentration camp. Finally, 'The Ark of Proletarian alliance was lost between Angola and Abyssinia' (near the remains of She).

These years were marked by events nearer France. Solzhenitsyn's *Gulag Archipelago* placed the brand of *Gulag* on the Soviet Union and thereby all 'real socialism'. In the petrol crisis of 1973, all the philosophies of desire which May 1968 had generated came to ground on reality.

In response intellectual life experienced a new birth in which almost everything had to be relearnt. On account of the rebirth Morin was indulgent even to false starts such as the appearance of the 'nouveaux philosophes', when a group of extreme Left leaders from *Mai '68* seemed to be signing publishing contracts and renouncing Marxism simultaneously, allegedly as a marketing ploy. The publications of this group of repentant Leftists at least announced a re-engagement with complexity. In philosophy and political theory, interrogation, freed from the tyranny of a syncretic structure, was soon renewed, but in the human sciences Morin accepted that epistemo-structuralism had proved more tenacious. Morin's perception of this tenacity is so intertwined with his own concerns that it characterises his messianic drive.

Epistemo-structuralism, he insisted, had fomented conceptual dementia: it reduced the human sciences to parts of a single determinist chain of invariant laws and yet prohibited any 'commerce' between the sciences on the other. Moved by the model of structural linguistics it asked each science to give itself an object, to isolate itself in a field so that even the particular human sciences could not legitimately communicate.

If communication was to flow the French intelligentsia had to learn that science rests not on certainty but the absence of certainty while France's philosophers of science had to further refine their understanding of science so as to abandon the 'idea of a clear demarcation between science and non-science (since on the contrary science had to be immersed in the non-scientific and the non-rational).'[30]

The institutional source of epistemo-structuralism's living death, its refusal to become ashes, Morin ascribed to the self-enclosed world of the French university system. Enclosed in its disciplinary bastions the intelligentsia modelled human sciences on structural linguistics and proved to be blithely unaware that such structuralism derived from an out-of-date Newtonian physics.

So the dissolution of the structuralist bastions required a process of inundation from outside (outside France) and from inside. Even the inundation from outside involved Morin indirectly since it invoked the Anglo-American influx of his desires. The translation of Popper's *The Logic of Scientific Discovery* was cited by Morin as a major event shifting French culture towards indeterminism; the assertion will be shown to be most open to debate.

*Messiah?*

The French works Morin listed demonstrate that he saw himself as orchestrator or organiser in a crusade since these works were all those of allies or preceded from colloquia presided by Morin. The list includes Monod's *Le Hasard et la Nécessité (Chance and Necessity*, Jacob's *La Logique du Vivant (The Logic of Living Systems)*, Prigogine and Stengers' *La Nouvelle Alliance*, Atlan's *Entre le crystal et la fumée* as well as the publications of the Royaumont Centre and a colloquium at Cerisy on self-organisation devoted to Morin. Morin often ironises about appearing to be a 'crusader': at Cerisy he called himself 'messie, mais non'. The irony indicates the magnitude of the messianic persona.[31]

Why has it had considerable success? My answer so far has combined his flamboyant self-obsession with the energy of his break with Marxism and now leads to the cultural predicament of the French Left, since what collapsed was not only Marxism as a theory but the culture of revolutionary brotherhood on which it rode. Now this culture was also one of brotherhood as a revolutionary community. And precisely because Morin is hugely self-certain in his repudiation of a theory, or its personalities, and of their cultural fields, he could become a judge, but also the provider of an alternative, after the multiple deaths of Big Brother. This was only possible because the alternative method he undertook did come to terms with intellectual difficulties ignored by epistemo-structuralism. The cultural function made possible by Morin's intellectual achievement is to liberate brotherhood from revolutionary socialism. The full ambiguity of this rescue is already expressed by the engraving on the frontispiece of this volume: fraternity remains steeped in the mythologies of revolution. Dating from the French Revolution the engraving seems to affirm fraternity as a relation between all humans but actually raises doubts as to the reality of the bond. The white female figure who symbolises and protects the revolutionary brotherhood between the white and the black male infants may be an allegory of the power of revolution to transcend biology but she can be their mother only allegorically, not biologically, so leaving open the question of how the allegory can be realised. Morin's answer to the realisation of fraternity hinges upon the successive deaths of Big Brother, the first of which is Morin's break with communism; the second France's break with Marxism, and the third the implosions of communism in 1989 and 1991 (see chapter 9).

It will also require a perception of fraternity as a 'mythico-real' relationship rooted in life 'herself' where the struggle between brothers is given a universal and egalitarian significance (see chapters 6 and 8).

The break with communism and the break with Marxism were fused in Morin's 'Damascus experience' of 1969–70. Now this did not prevent him from integrating his past into *La Méthode* but it did free him to pass an apocalyptic judgement on French Marxism years before the apocalypse. It would be easy to construct an alternative history of Marxism in France and to insist on its intellectual fertility and 'bio-diversity'. It is egocentrism which allows Morin to believe that the suicide of *Arguments* closed Marxism to innovation.

In the years after 1962 the interrelationship of existential Marxism and structuralist Marxism, including the virulence of Althusser's attack on Sartre, was experienced as an intellectual adventure. The age of structuralist Marxism was then one of vigorous battles (see Henri Lefebvre's attacks on Althusser) both inside and outside France. The excitement of May 1968 was enhanced by the feeling that Althusser the priest and Sartre the prophet had joined to crown Leftism as a new king. Indeed on the eve of conversion Morin himself sensed as much. An entry in *Californie* (late 1969) records his decision to sign a petition for the liberation of Régis Debray and adds, 'I had troubled feeling towards (Régis) when he took the path Sartre–Althusser–Fidel offered him, although I offered him the path of *Arguments*; yet I know there is no path of *Arguments*.'[32] The converse is crucial: after 1970 there would be a path of Edgar Morin in which name he could act with crusading self-confidence.

That Morin grossly overstated the function of Marxism as an episteme (mind set) and hence the marginality of non-Marxist strands in pre-1975 French intellectual activity, became part of his cultural power. Morin's crusade mobilised many 'marginal' lines of enquiry. Moreover because his own intellectual activity was uniquely self-referential, he quickly seized on the almost biologically self-destructive personal tragedies which permeated the final years of Marxist dominance.

In the face of several acts of 'Dostoevskian' moral self-destruction, Morin led by 'rashly' saying the unsayable. A notorious instance came when Althusser, who, but for the grace of Marx, might well have become a Catholic priest, in 1981 killed his Jewish spouse. Morin jumped in and said what was then ridiculed and is now admitted, namely: 'Sometime before the tragedy, Althusser had ceased to believe all he taught (as a Marxist) but dared not publish his doubts.'[33]

Thus Morin had begun with a radically Promethean interpretation of Hegelian Marxism; he transformed this into an approach to science which would be proof against determinism; such change would rule out not only structuralist schemes but the Hegelian historicism of his youth. The cultural attraction of Morin's path was its commitment to the values of the 'intelligentsia de gauche'.

In Morin's vision the Left is rescued as a legitimate myth. Its inheritance, despite its uncertainties, is given the value of fraternity. Fraternity requires the death of *Big Brother*, that is, the aspiration to remodel societies towards fraternal perfection. Nevertheless it legitimates an inheritance of struggles and (male) bondings. It invites the Left to regard a new age of humanity as an inspiration but not a programme. But to sustain the aspiration as an adventure for the Left is also a way of protecting French traditions from onslaughts such as that of 'Anglo-Saxon feminism'. Morin's emphasis on fraternity as both male and universal is echoed by the stubborn adherence within the Left intelligentsia to *femininity*. To peruse *L'Infini* (the journal of Kristeva) suggests that France, the 'mother' of feminist theory, has in the name of the feminine rejected the lifestyles and the theories of her Anglo-American 'daughters', that is, all the physical, dress and linguistic behaviour we call political correctness. (Political correctness is widely seen in France as a denial/fear of difference. French is a systematically masculine–feminine language in which nothing can be said without gender reference; a gender neutral version would be a great change, one likely to be denounced as anglophone cultural imperialism.)

### *Translating Morin*

All translators agree translation is 'impossible': each language is weighed by its own culture and history and each author has a unique relationship to this inheritance. In the case of Morin I have suggested his war with the academic establishment makes him more not less peculiarly French in English eyes. His crusade permeates his highly personalised style. Its most colourful feature is the creation of neologisms formed by accumulating prefixes: sometimes the string of prefixes is like an extended DNA chain, as in Morin's definition of life, (Auto (géno-phéno-égo-éco-re-organisation-computationnelle-informationelle-communicationnelle)). The concept itself will be analysed in chapter 6. Syntactically the expression is a solvent in which the isolated identities of its components are dissolved.

Because Morin's intellectual objective is to subvert the pervasive rationalism of French intellectual culture, his style bears its imprint as a negative or shadow. No word is more crucial to this symbiosis of a ruling culture with its guerrillas than *logique*. It is only in dictionaries that English logic and *logique* coincide. I shall indicate Morin's use of *logique* by translating it as 'logic'. The point of the quotation marks is to indicate that *logique*, much more than 'logical', is used to mean not only deductive logic but also development, force or historical consequence. 'Complex thought' struggles to escape the imprisoning power of the words *logique* and *raison* by exploiting their complexity.

CHAPTER 2

# Morin in the Communist Underworld

In 1959 Morin published *Autocritique*, an autobiography which was also the first cultural anthropology of communist intellectuals in France. The title exposed the themes of the book and, I argue, proved a key to the culture of existential Marxism. It set Morin on his path of self-examination. The word 'autocritique' has entered the English language. It denotes self-criticism, particularly by communists, and connotes a situation of being on trial. The connotation is crucial. *Autocritique* was organised around the threat and shadow of trial. It was pervaded by a guilt which Morin was not to resolve until 1956, if then, since the guilt was multifaceted: it included both the error of having been a Stalinist and of betraying communism.

As an exploration of the trial atmosphere of the PCF, *Autocritique* conjoined a sociology or cultural anthropology of intellectuals in the PCF with that of existential Marxism in France. The connection was dramatically represented through Morin's own experience of being on trial. There were two such moments in *Autocritique*: the first came as a repercussion of the trial of the communist leader Laszlo Rajk in Hungary in 1949, the second was the rite of expulsion Morin incurred in 1951. In these experiences he was able to identify himself and his fellow dissident intellectuals in the PCF as 'the existentialists of Marxism' and, reciprocally, to illuminate the imagery of trial at the heart of a generation of French intellectuals.

*Autocritique's* exploration of the themes of identity concerned not only Morin, French communist intellectuals and the generation of existential Marxism, but the root of their identities in French political culture.[1] Such a dramatised exploration gave *Autocritique* an illuminating force in French intellectual life in a way which theoretical 'critiques' of existential Marxism could not attain.[2] *Autocritique* was exceptional in revealing how ultimate, 'existential' decisions whether to affirm or disavow communism depended on the play of identities. By his subjective approach Morin could indicate why existential Marxism had two versions: the more famous 'signed' Merleau-Ponty and Sartre and the one directly experienced by communist intellectuals.[3] He could also show why the more famous version was tributary to that of these 'existentialists of Marxism'.

I argue that the story of *Autocritique* reveals how communism was initially essential but became an impediment to Morin's identity as 'Morin' and as French. Since I read the story to expose its subordinate but not subconscious theme of identity, I depart from Morin's chronological sequence. I start with his Marxist ideology so as to see how it first saved, then threatened, Morin's identity and why Morin had to leave by helping stage a symbolic trial.

## *Stalinism made Reasonable*

When Morin joined the PCF in 1942 he came under the spell of a version of communism commonly termed Hegelian Marxism: to indicate its ubiquity among the intellectuals of his group, if not generation, *Autocritique* called it 'the vulgate'. The principal thinker of the group was a Hungarian, Szekeres, who had in turn learnt his Marxism from Lukacs. Indeed so much was Hegelian Marxism indebted to Lukacs that one could term it Lukacs communism.

The vulgate was *not* existential Marxism but it was so tuned to individual experience as to take the colour of existentialism through the impact of events. Ideologically the vulgate was a mystique which made 'the Party's' members freely reasoning judges of 'the Party's' decisions whilst always acquiescing in its politics. They saw themselves as 'a-political', that is, concerned with the ideological significance but indifferent to the political strategies of communism.

The mystique degraded Lukacs' concept of praxis whereby the proletariat rationally directed historical processes by its ability to unify theory and practice. But in the vulgate praxis came to signify the individual Party member's ability to rationalise lucidly the political decisions of 'the Party'. The organisational process behind this version of Lukacs combined the Stalinist concentration of political decision-making in the Party apparatus (and ultimately Moscow) with the sense of heroism and moral autonomy French communism acquired in the Resistance. Its ideological outcome was the confidence of the vulgate intellectuals that they 'knew the facts', despite their indifference to details of information.

In Hegelian terminology their personal autonomy was underwritten by a 'dialectic of truth and error'. Truth was guaranteed by a determinism in which the Party, acting on behalf of the proletariat and working for a socialist economy, must be right.[5] But this left the vulgate intellectuals free to perceive error in 'the Party's' historically assured movement towards truth.

Linguistically Morin caught this 'a-political' confidence by playing on the related senses of the word 'la Raison' which can denote reason, rationality and right while connoting all three. The opportunity to distinguish between reason as 'being right' and reason as 'broadly reasonable' whilst also combining these senses enabled Morin to justify his 'a-political' communism by exploiting its congruence with a Hegelianism buried inside the French language itself.

> We did not think that the party 'avait toujours raison' [literally 'was always right']. We thought that the party 'était dans la raison' [literally 'was within the bounds of reason' but in context 'on the right path']. Like 'la Raison' [reason itself] journeying through the ages the party could stumble.[6]

The psychological consequence of such a 'mutilated' (that is, 'a political') praxis was almost magical. For being 'a-political' the intellectuals of the vulgate could identify themselves with 'the Party' and yet place responsibility for its decisions elsewhere: they could attribute personal decisions to different circumstances distanced from themselves either in time (the past, the future) or by geography. It was not inevitable, but it is understandable, why the events which destroyed the vulgate were such as to force Morin to confront his personal responsibility for Party political decisions and thereby discover that he was an 'existentialist of Marxism'. Hence the significance of the psychology of being on trial for Morin, since it would mirror the real trials which Stalin made into the centrepiece of communist organisation and culture.

So the moment of truth for Morin came when the Rajk trial began to affect him personally in mid-1949. The first event was that Szekeres, an associate of Rajk, was recalled to Hungary. Morin and his wife, Violette, saw him off.

> He was still thinking of the book he wished to write, *The Individual Facing History*; but 'History' wrote this book instead of him.[7]

We can say of *Autocritique* that *it* was the book 'History' wrote; it finally put Morin on trial and acquitted him. But as long as he was a communist this was impossible except by proxy. Indeed the problem could only be publicly aired by proxy. The book of such an act of ventriloquy, much discussed in Morin's circle, Merleau-Ponty's *Humanism and Terror*, appeared in 1947. Unfortunately Merleau-Ponty condemned communist intellectuals to heroic self-abnegation. Merleau-Ponty, who was not a communist, but used the principles of a-political communism, concluded that a communist who 'knew the facts' must in all circumstances accept the Party's judgement upon himself:[8] for the a-political communist, this implied the tragic freedom of accepting self-mutilation while knowing its true significance.

The dramatic structuring of *Autocritique* around Morin's involvement in and experience of being on trial thus captured the sense in which he and his comrades were 'existentialists of Marxism'. The trial in such a context was the moment of truth not only intellectually but as a personal and political destiny. The Vulgate intellectuals were intellectually committed to but personally unprepared for their role.

The personal destiny was almost unavoidable because communism in the Stalin era had become a political culture in which trial and confession were promoted as a key dramatic device: Jean Duvignaud, Morin's future collaborator in *Arguments,* later termed the Stalin trials communism's greatest contribution to world theatre.[9] But until the Rajk trial hit them, the intellectuals of the vulgate could deal with the Moscow trials by employing Merleau-Ponty's schema while believing that it did not affect them personally.

Merleau-Ponty's explanation as to why Stalin's lieutenants confessed involved making praxis an exercise in comprehension. He proposed a 'wager on history' which would accommodate both her deviousness and her rationality (history for Merleau-Ponty became a *femme fatale*). The wager was available only to communists. Indeed only between communists could a bet be placed knowing that human action would express Reason in the most unforeseen dark mists of public events. The confessional mode of all the evidence at the Moscow trials presented an opportunity to demonstrate the significance of personal responsibility in politics. Merleau-Ponty thus declared that the leading victim of the third trial, Bukharin, had explained his responsibility for action which in a non-political court he could have repudiated. For Merleau-Ponty Bukharin was both Socrates and saint of communism, sacrificing himself as an educational act.

Merleau-Ponty did not aspire to sanctity. In terms of an existentialist morality his interpretation was equivalent to the physical division of a single city by a Berlin wall. Only on the communist side of the wall were intellectuals fully privileged to decipher the messages of History. Non-communist intellectuals were condemned to be their ventriloquists.

Morin and his fellow intellectuals read *Humanism and Terror* with a sense of security. They experienced the principle of a praxis available only to communists as an indelible seal; while they incarnated praxis, others, at best, mimicked them. All that Merleau-Ponty attributed to Bukharin they attributed to themselves but they felt as safe as was Merleau-Ponty. The risks of praxis belonged to other circumstances and in another country.

After the war Morin believed the confessional trials belonged to an unrepeatable ice age. There had been three major public trials known thereafter as the Moscow trials. Between August 1936 and March 1938 60 communists accused themselves of lifelong treachery to Communism. But these trials then stopped. The second series, of which the Rajk trial was the first, only began in September 1949. Retrospectively, in *Autocritique*, Morin could see that there had been two ice ages and that his vulgate communism, far from expressing deliverance from trial, had been an inter-ice-age phenomenon.[10] But the vulgate, having isolated the first ice age as a unique event, attributed to the Second World War the character of a definitive watershed.

The material symbol of this rupture was the battle of Stalingrad. For Morin Stalingrad would fuse the transition from an age of barbarism to one of unlimited hope in his own liberation from the fear-ridden identities of prewar France.

Stalingrad united the end of barbarism to the regeneration of France and of Edgar Morin under the sign of Stalin. The vulgate was not only Hegelo-Marxism but Hegelo-Stalinism.[11] For Morin the real Stalin had not stood up until 'Stalingrad'.

## *The Hour of Stalingrad*

The barbaric struggle against barbarism undertaken by the prewar Soviet state found its counterpoint in the cultural diminution suffered by prewar France as well as the personal despair of the adolescent Morin since, at the time, he, like many French, could see only barbarism.

Morin's memory of the late 1930s was that of a period in which all his horizons were shrinking. The Soviet Union, a 'steel condor', complemented Nazism's voodoo as a force working to crush France and Morin. In such a world communism was not to the Left but to the barbarous east of France.

The France of the late 1930s had lost her universal, fraternal mission; in the midst of a 'world encircled by the tom-tom of death' France could only desperately search to hide from barbarism. Morin's connection in 1939 with the anarcho-syndicalist journal *La Flèche*, an ember from the nationalist anarchism of Proudhon and Sorel, bore witness to the implosion of his adolescent aspirations towards cosmic and human brotherhood.[12] 'One had to work on the level of human reality. My horizon did not stretch beyond France ... I feared I would die before I had lived.'[13]

The sense of mutilation, of ideology as a castrating force external to France, was agonizingly intensified by the Nazi victory. Morin could only hope that barbarism would ultimately work for civilisation even if the price were 'the immolation of the Jews if the salvation of France so required'.[14] These images allow us to add the sense of national liberation to Morin's subsequent feeling that to join the Communist Party was a 'reconciliation with oneself and the world'.[15] After Stalingrad the images of isolated France in a world of darkness could be reversed. At the liberation in 1944 'we communists incarnated the will of the French people' and Morin himself became a 'repentant anti-Stalinist, sitting astride two generations'.[16]

Morin could recognise that in resolving his conflicts of self in action he had also solved the cultural identity of his self. To be French was not to suffer being mutilated but to be part of an order of communication in the triumphant advance of socialism. Morin's solution was partly private to the intellectuals of the vulgate if not to himself. His vision of France was almost bound to germinate into a politics of cultural opposition: the 'a-political' distance from practical politics would have a dual function: it masked the virulence of the discord and at the same time fed the cultural dimension in which Morin would find himself at odds with the communist movement both in its French and its international directions.

## *The A-Political Dissidents*

The dialectic of truth and error played with the Party line in such a way that Morin diverged while hardly noticing where or even that he was drifting. It was not until 1947 that he began to take stock of his differences.

A hostile critic could say of Morin's a-political communism, 'But you were never a communist'; and we could concede that he had not a 'naturally communist soul'.

France between 1944 and 1946, for him and his companions of the Vulgate, was a house of many cafés. He mixed with a wide range of intellectuals: the atheists (Sartre and Camus), the quasi-atheists (Merleau-Ponty), and especially with progressivist Catholics.[17] Only later, writing *Autocritique,* did he comprehend that to a Stalinist inquisitor he was a deviationist in the bud, and that he deviated both Left and Right of the Party line.[18] The fraternalism of the 'a-political' stance was to the left of a strategy which sought to exploit a quite unfraternal nationalism which fused anti-German hatred with Jacobin and quasi-Bonapartist desires to remain an imperial power. But Morin's vulgate was more fundamentally to the right of the PCF because 'a-politically' he exaggerated the surface appearance of French communism's ideological autonomy from the Soviet model. Morin adopted Friedmann's formula that the Soviet Union was an example not a model, although Friedmann was only a syndicalist sympathiser to communism. In 1946 Thorez, the Party leader Morin respected, told *The Times* of London that France would find her own path to socialism. Morin decided to theorise this path relying on the 'ontological' break between the ages of barbarism and reconciliation. He submitted an article to *Action*, journal of the Resistance intellectuals, in which he distinguished between the proletarian dictatorship necessitated by the harshness of the prewar age and the proletarian domination which the Second World War had established in the people's democracies of Eastern Europe and which was now possible in France. Submitted in November 1946, the article was refused as 'revisionist' but, comically, Morin could not see his own revisionism.[19] According to the vulgate he had simply theorised what the Party was really doing.

The two faces of Morin's deviation expressed his assumption that communism had entered an age where it could directly practise the politics of 'total man', a communism entirely liberated from its own barbarous prehistory. Such an assumption was not only 'ontological' and 'a-political' but it also articulated the vulgate's expectations about how a culturally liberated France would function. Now Morin's vision of the identity of France was 'unknown' to him, quite at odds with the nationalist agendas of Soviet communism and its consequences for the PCF, so that 'Living in culture I was brought to a cultural opposition.'[20]

In 1947 Morin's closest associates were the writers Robert Antelme, ex-concentration camp inmate, Dionys Mascolo and Marguerite Duras, then married to Mascolo.[21] In that year the 'second glaciation' began to bite. The feature which most differentiated it from the first Stalinist glaciation was the pre-eminence it accorded to cultural and national identities. Thus, when, as Morin wrote, 'We believed with a stupid pride and naïve relief that our opposition had nothing in common with prewar political oppositions such as Trotskyism',[22] this belief was almost an inversion of a Party line which sought to define communist loyalties in a Byzantine game of national essences.

In 1947 the name which above all others was associated with this germinating inquisition was that of Andrei Zhdanov, Stalin's first lieutenant in the Soviet Communist Party. From the existence of only two camps (communist and imperialist) Zhdanov concluded that all contemporary culture was either communist or anti-communist and, in the latter case, decadent. Zhdanov joined to this explicit principle of exclusion an implicit hierarchy: the highest achievements of socialist culture were those of the Russian, Soviet people.

The effect of the Zhdanov report in France was to strengthen the PCF's version of this implicit hierarchy. The Russian people were more perfect in socialism than any other: the French more perfect than any but the Russians.[23]

The Hegelo-Stalinism of the dissidents was thus the negative image not only of Zhdanovism but of its PCF variant. Their post-Stalingrad Stalin was the emblem of redemptive power not of a principle of exclusion. The cultural identities they sought for France were expansive, whereas Zhdanovism and the PCF seemed bent on enclosing them in a ghetto – as had existed in the 1930s. Thus their cultural skirmishes made them more 'Hegelian' – they invoked the total man of Hegelian Marxism against the actual practices of their party.

The skirmishes of 1947–8 ran along two interconnected fronts: 'Against' Zhdanov, Morin defended fallen writers such as Gide. Against the chauvinism of the PCF.[24] Morin and Mascolo maintained close ties with the Italian communist Elio Vittorini.[25] It was a perceived mark of Italian communism to accord culture a relatively autonomous standing and for several months Morin and Mascolo engaged in a low-level guerrilla action by elevating 'Vittorinism' as a banner. The Party leadership in the person of Laurent Casanova, the director of ideology, was not deceived: 'What is this Italian up to, giving lessons to us, the French?' he asked (Casanova was a Corsican).[26]

The tremors of an opposition which believed itself purified of political content were smothered in June 1948 when the Kominform proclaimed Tito's Yugoslavia a fascist ally of the Americans. The vulgate could operate to ratify such analyses by betting on history: Morin and Mascolo agreed that Tito was a lesser Stalin and therefore the greater Stalin had to be chosen against his miniature.[27] But the excommunication of Tito was not only 'political': it brought back 'The Stalinism of the trials and the purges'; based on 'the magical thinking and the structures of the Church' it crystallised into black magic.[28] The ultimate inversion took place within the PCF itself for in France the religious magic became the infrastructure of terror.

> In the PCF terror could not be policed ... since we were under no material constraints ... it was psychological (exclusion, betrayal) a face of the sacred, of the love we bore to the Party-of-the-Proletariat. We were believers who tremble before the God of Love.[29]

Commenting on Stalinism from the distance of 1959, Morin felt entitled to see a dialectical vindication of his 'a-political communism'.

> Our extraordinarily late political critique ... was finally more radical than any political critique. It started from epiphenomena, emotional revolt, refusal of reason but slowly took our entire being.[30]

But, I argue, Morin's political backwardness of 1948 left its mark by the use of political circumstances to stage symbolic trials which would return a 'not guilty' verdict.

In 1948–9 Morin could only experience his 'Titoism' as if struck dumb. His accusers said he was a Titoist since Morin frequented ex-communists such as Duvignaud who had expelled themselves by visiting Yugoslavia. He met the Trotskyist Gilles Martinet who told him of Soviet economic exploitation in the people's democracies. But he hid within his a-political fatalism. He wrote nothing about Tito, that is, nothing against Stalin.[31] This inner self would, however, be forced out of him.

## *An Afternoon in Hell*

By a meaningful coincidence the first of the 1949–52 confessional trials was held in Budapest. Morin had learnt his Marxism from Szekeres, and yet another Hungarian friend was François Fejto, then an official in the Hungarian embassy. Morin's friendships were the reverse image of a trial that was directed not only against Tito (and his Yankee puppet masters) but against the Marxism of Lukacs, friend of Szekeres and Fejto, creator of what scholars have subsequently termed 'Western Marxism'.[32] In July 1949 a fate like Szekeres' hung over Fejto. Fejto had left the Hungarian Communist Party in 1935. He had been closely connected to Rajk and they remained personal friends: both men came from the Westernised haute bourgeoisie of Budapest.[33] One day Fejto called Morin.

> The Hungarian information office occupied a lodge on the Rue Saint-Jacques. I hesitated before an empty staircase,and when confronted I asked for Fejto.
>
> Fejto alone in an office began an incomprehensible discourse ... When someone entered he stopped ... Finally he could explain ... He had received a telegram recalling him in 24 hours.
>
> I was in an extraterritorial fragment in the heart of the Latin Quarter. Through the window I could see the leaves of the trees rustle gently. But the huge shadow of a police hell hovered over us. It was a psychic, mental trap, or rather a mad house where the guardians were mad. Fejto was riveted to his desk. We must leave I said. In the street, things regained their usual shape but the other universe floated around. I had lived two hours like a phantom invulnerable to its laws. We drank beer on the terrace.
>
> My friends, my brothers, myself were henceforth the prey of this police [but] I was in France.[34]

The contrast between the normality of France and an alien Eastern police state was articulated through Morin's images. The action began in the reassuring Latin quarter and ended with a beer on a terrace. In between was a world of silent, whispering, feverish, incomprehensible phantoms against whom France was a golden bough: the visible rustle of trees ensured Morin's safety. The topological contrast displayed the magic power of a police apparatus: Fejto himself had been incomprehensible inside the embassy while

Morin, like Fejto, had brothers 'over there'. The magic of the police state worked inside France, certainly inside the PCF and even within Morin himself. It would leave Morin haunted by a dominant theme: culture and barbarism, communication and noise are in his work always symbiotic. Seated before his beer Morin had escaped existentially but not yet ideologically.

Nevertheless his golden bough had become grounded in an irreversible decision: he had entered 'hell' and saved Fejto.

And so, I argue, while he remained inside the PCF he began to grow invulnerable to its laws.

Psychologically Morin began to observe his fellow communists almost as if he were Dante visiting the Dead. The most fallen of these undead was Pierre Courtade, whose self-immolation would define for Morin the historical function of the Rajk trial: it would be the moment of judgement for the vulgate intellectuals. Courtade was a late comer to the PCF. 'I was not a Communist in 1944 because I was in Russia before the war', he often said. His moment of decision, like Morin's, was thrust upon him. Sent to Budapest as a reporter for *L'Humanité*, he did more than write the required articles. He believed. 'I feared this would be a charade like the Moscow trials, but no, Rajk really was a spy', he insisted and referred to material proofs he had almost been shown.[35]

What did Courtade really believe? – Morin asked himself and his remaining friends. In *Autocritique* he concluded that Courtade was his double.

After 1946 Courtade split into a public and a private persona: 'his extreme intelligence exemplified the cynicism and religion ... of the mystics-cynics'.[36]

Due precisely to his extravagant subjectivism Morin had expressed a widespread anguish among pro-Marxist intellectuals,[37] a dialectic of faith and doubt which became public with the return of the trials. Such moments of decision occurred throughout the French Left intelligentsia in a way which vindicated Morin's description of his group as the 'existentialists of Marxism': the instance I shall give concerns the catholic existentialists of the journal *Esprit*.

The decision by *Esprit* to publish Fejto's article on the Rajk trial in November 1949 was taken in self-torment and produced a stormy onslaught on Jean Lacroix, one of its guardian spirits, by his former student Louis Althusser. Lacroix reiterated the voice of his conscience: he had to allow Fejto's witness to be heard, despite Althusser's argument which 'proved' Rajk's CIA connections by the logic of class war.[38]

The importance of the acts of witnessing in *Autocritique* I suggest was one element in the existential-Marxist intellectuals' perception of the confessional trials rather than the concentration camps as the essential face of Stalinism. Certainly this was so for Morin. The mounting evidence of a concentration camp universe intensified without transforming the sense of a world in dementia. He remained a communist: on the ideological level the vulgate could still function to integrate the concentration camps into the socialist project and destiny of the Soviet Union. In what Morin termed the fourth dimension of subjectivity we encounter a striking contrast between two sorts of memory. The details of his involvement with the Rajk trial were remembered by Morin as if in a three-dimensional video: the two hours in the Hungarian embassy, even the words and gestures of Courtade or Pierre Hervé – with whom he argued – are all etched in *Autocritique* in an extended present tense. In contrast Morin reconstructed his response to the concentration camps with, 'I would like to recall my internal debate relating to the Soviet camps.'[39]

## *Expulsion*

'I thought my contradictions were heroic whereas they were Freudian,'[40] Morin wrote of the two years after July 1949 when he still remained a communist. Symbolic sexual roles abound: 'the Party' was super-ego, mother, spouse and lover. Morin played out these roles in a Sartrean strategy of bad faith. His unacknowledged agenda was to force an outcome of his 'bet on history' and challenge 'the Party' to expel him: when, in 1951, he suffered expulsion, the suffering was both passive and active.

Intellectually he appealed to Hegel against Marxism, to Marxism against Stalinism: hence his suspicion that he was merely yielding to the promptings of 'the beautiful soul, moralism and ethics ... Morally I rejected the system but ideologically I rejected my morality.'[41]

In existential terms, however, the real decision had already been taken. While Morin hung onto the Communist Party as a prophylactic against nihilism, another faith, that of science, initially of Marxism as a 'depoliticised' science, was growing.

Morin's expulsion took the guise of a trial he helped to stage. Unable to desert ('like a rat'), in December 1949 he found a solution which condensed communism into a metaphysical essence: he failed to renew his Party card for 1950 but continued to 'consider myself a party member'.[42] Unemployed since his refusal of the post of literary critic for *L'Humanité* in 1948, Morin found his path when he began to write *L'Homme* in 1949. Cocooned in his work he sought to combine Marx and Freud: 'There was no taboo over me.'[43] On the contrary: he found taboos to break. His first article in sociology was a conference report for the Trotskyist *L'Observateur*. He was asked if he wished it to appear signed and answered, 'no problem'.[44]

In the spring of 1951 the secretary of the Seine federation, Annie Besse (later, as Annie Kriegel, France's leading analyst of the PCF) summoned him. She was 'blonde, icy and innocent'.[45]

'What do you think of a communist who writes for the intelligence service?' Morin denied knowing that *L'Observateur* was a journal of the intelligence service. 'What gave you the right to insult our great comrade Mao?' Morin had mentioned Mao's exclusion from the Third International: this, he pointed out, was stated in Mao's memoirs which had appeared in a PCF journal. 'What are you doing at present?' 'A book on death ... from a Marxist standpoint.' He had not, he further admitted, consulted the PCF's experts.

Some days later he was asked by a comrade to the cell meeting. Most were workers ... they seemed to be waiting for someone. Annie Besse entered. She demanded Morin's exclusion. She explained that he had written for a journal of the CIA and that he was at the CNRS under Friedmann, 'renegade and apostle of police sociology'.

Morin in his defence insisted that his ideological differences were ancient and well known:

> 'I denied all political disagreement.'
> 'The expulsion was voted unanimously.'
> 'I brayed like a newly born ... Eight days later I was happy, unburdened and joyous.'

Morin used his freedom to continue as he was: the a-political communist became an a-political ex-communist. Had Annie Besse read *L'Homme* she would have found a Marxist critique of Marxist-Stalinism. After expulsion Morin made his approach in *L'Homme* explicit. In an unpublished article he declared that the task of the intellectual was to construct a 'communist anthropology' which, chapter 3 of this book argues, is what *L'Homme* already represented.[46]

On several occasions – the last in February 1956 when Mikoyan absolved the victims of the Moscow trials accused of treason and espionage – Morin believed that communism might return to its human root of total liberation.

The definitive end came with Khrushchev's secret speech and the uprisings in Poland and Hungary – all in 1956. Khrushchev's speech claimed a detail which struck at the heart of the existential Marxism created by Merleau-Ponty: most of the confessions were extracted by torture.[47]

A self-evident question can be put. Why did Morin decide torture in the real trials blew away the relevance of existentialist torments when his own story so strikingly exemplified the power of the imagery and psychology of trial? On the contrary, I suggest, Morin's story of a 'mythico-real' trial explains more about Stalinist trials than the 'fact' of torture, the lowest common denominator of all police states; the Second World War, moreover, demonstrated how often Communists could resist Nazi torture. But Khrushchev's revelations gave Morin certainty at last that his decision to be expelled had been heroic not sentimental. When Khrushchev 'killed' Big Brother he made possible Morin's adventure into fraternity of which *Arguments* was first fruit.

CHAPTER 3

# Amortality: Morin's Marxist Myth

In *L'Homme* (1951) Morin first staked a claim to envelop the social sciences and biology. In chapter 2 we saw how this work surreptitiously expressed the trauma of leaving 'the Party'. At the time its position at a crossroad between Marxist theory and philosophy of science combined with the dominance of Marxism in French culture so as to surround it with a penumbra of misunderstanding. Morin's political subservience hid his intellectual boldness: in exploring the Hegelian Marxist emphasis on the satisfaction of need he affirmed that Marxism demanded from science the indefinite extension of life he termed 'amortality'. It was seen that *L'Homme* was Marxist and mythic but not how the myth was an *autocritique* of Marxism.

In the 1960s Morin ceased to subscribe to amortality and he ceased to consider himself a Marxist: hence I term amortality Morin's Marxist myth. Moreover the extreme length to which Morin pushed Marxism's promise to abolish need helps explain his prominence in the debates which exposed the conflicts of existential Marxism and his subsequent indifference to the structuralist versions of Marxism in which the suppression of need is itself suppressed.

In adding the adjective Marxist to Morin's subsequent characterisation of amortality as a myth I shall, however, stay close to Morin's own understanding of myth. Myth, in my analysis, is a story which depicts a human or cosmic order.

This narrative can be reasonably accurate or a blatant legend. Morin would later devise the expression 'mythico-real' to indicate the complex relationship of such stories to reality. In this sense even science can be bearer of a myth, as, Morin argues, is the case with cosmological theories, notably the 'big bang' (see chapter 5).

The story of *L'Homme* was that of the conquest of death by science, a conquest which, being scientific, Morin termed amortality, the scientifically possible version of immortality. Whereas an immortal being, invulnerable to death, is a supernatural entity, amortality is merely the progressive dissolution of limits to the life span. Amortality might be in the realm of science fiction but precisely for that reason remains a scientific speculation. Nevertheless from the standpoint of 'mere' mortals the two form a continuum; in the eyes of common sense the difference is as blurred as a theological distinction.

Ideologically this story functioned to demonstrate the depth of Marx's Hegelian inheritance. The audacity of 'young Morin' was such that Georges Bataille, his most alert reader, said he was 'walking on eggs'.[1] To minimise the shock Morin held back his explicit acknowledgement of Marx as 'author' of the myth. The outcome was that amortality became the unconscious demand of Marx and Marxism, with Morin the myth maker of Marxism.

*L'Homme* divided into five sections of which the first was a 'genetic anthropology'. The expression 'anthropology' to denote generic humanity stamped this section as derived from the 1844 manuscripts of Marx, but the names of Marx and Hegel only emerged on the penultimate page. Sections two, three and four explored the historical-ideological stages through which humanity sought to assuage the trauma of death. The final section, the 'struggle against death' envisaged the possibility that science would give a material resolution to a trauma which magic, religion and philosophy could only assuage with fantasies or ideologies. Here, at last, Marx took centre stage and was theatrically established as the centrepiece of Morin's myth.

## *The Anthropology of Need*

In the language of Marxism the expression 'anthropology' is used to affirm the unity of all human sciences while rejecting the existence of a fixed human nature. When Hegelian Marxists denied the existence of human nature in the name of anthropology they could be construed to mean that human nature was unlimitable and protean in its capacities. Only in the last section of *Man and Death L'Homme* would Morin produce the quotations from which stemmed his interpretation of Marx's materialism as a faith in the practical energies whereby man could satisfy all the needs which his own humanity generated. He joined two famous (or notorious) passages; one from the 1844 manuscripts, the other from the theses on Feuerbach. In 1844 Marx had already said:

> The solution of theoretical oppositions is possible only in practice, by human energy, and this solution ... is a real and vital task, which philosophy could not solve, precisely because it only saw a theoretical task.

The theses on Feuerbach thence derived a super-optimistic aphorism, 'Humanity only asks the questions it can solve.'[2]

Materialism in this sense could be understood as the pragmatic converse of Hegel's idealism, that is, as the effective, hence real, appropriation of all the human needs whose satisfaction Hegel conceived only as the work of philosophy. Morin took so much for granted when he wrote that his method was that of Hegel but above all Marx.[3] Mascolo argued this position in *Le Communisme* of 1953.[4]

Hegel, Mascolo said, had grasped human nature as the satisfaction of desire by the labour of intellect. Marx's revolution was simplicity itself since, by insisting on the materiality of the means of satisfying desire, Marx 'materialised' desire as need. Hence Mascolo argued, human nature did not exist except as the total materialisation of human needs.

Mascolo's interpretation was a 'materialist' counterpart to negative theology: man is only to be defined by what he is not. But precisely for this reason Mascolo refused to ask, as Morin did, 'what do we need?'

In pressing the question which underlay the theology embedded in Hegelian Marxism, Morin exposed an empty space within it. For Marx had resolutely failed to consider the problem of death, whereas Hegel's *Phenomenology of Spirit* is crucially engaged in charting the path of true consciousness in the shadow of death.

Indeed the dialectic of master and slave, central to all French Hegelian Marxism, turns for Hegel around such consciousness of death. And yet, as Morin said, all Marx could provide was one cryptic remark in the 1844 manuscripts: to say that death did not rupture the unity of individual and species since the individual was only mortal appeared to accept Hegel's ultra-idealist resolution of the problem.[5]

Here was the first contradiction Morin would discern (as yet allusively) in Marxism. Marx had accepted that the individual, the bearer of need, had to be consummated – not cancelled out – by the material power of productive forces. Why then this silence about the challenge of death?

Implicitly Morin suggested production had become not only an end but an escape for Marxism. In terms of the satisfaction of need, man the producer had right of way only because his was the heroic and realistic resolution of needs. But Marxism entangled itself in its commitment to heroic realism so that it became an end in itself: 'any problem inaccessible to practice is insoluble and hence false for if it were real the real problem would be admittedly insoluble.'[6]

The mythological figure who embodied Marxism's hunger for realism and the danger of being trapped within it was that of Prometheus.[7] The Prometheus myth encoded the political culture, through which Marx and Marxism 'forgot' the 'insoluble problems' Marx originally posed. They immersed themselves in revolutionary praxis and thereby came to be entirely absorbed by the class struggle with all the interest it provided. The combination of productivism as a theory and its corollary of revolutionary praxis as culture entirely covered the nakedness of Marx's original insight.

In characterising the political culture Morin allowed himself to break cover: the darkness at the heart of Marxism he described was patently that of his own personal experience with the PCF and anticipated the drama of *Autocritique*:

> the Marxist *vulgate* has become a remedy against anguish, a new opium ... a ruse of reason whereby the individual must sacrifice himself to assure the victory of individuality ... it invokes the 'reign of instructible men', that is, victory over death, but ignores the painful fantasm, the sterile anguish before the insoluble.[8]

These lines recall Morin's sense of anguish; his response was to maintain an undiminished affirmation of Marx's utopianism.

## *Prometheus and the Vulture*

One way to walk on eggs is to employ metaphors. Morin exposed the tension between Marx's utopianism and his productivism by depicting humanity as a land with two passports: a scientific, valid passport, issued to 'man the toolmaker', and a passport without visa ... namely the grave.[9]

To integrate the contrast between the tool and the grave put back into question Marxism's faith in production: such faith had caused Marxism to lose sight of the question it originally posed about the nature of the human species. For this reason Morin termed his version of the dialectic 'progressive-regressive', since it brought back into play society's relationship to individual needs and beyond them the demarcation lines between the human species and its animal origin.[10] Such a regression not only redirected Marxism back to Marx but also 'back to Freud' since it re-examined the species relationship of man to animal, not in terms of productivity, but the terms of the psyche and its traumas. Describing man as the 'adapted-inadapted animal' Morin put inadaptation in place of the Hegelian Marxist concept of alienation. Inadaptation recalled the insistence of the classical French *moralistes* Pascal and La Rochefoucault especially, on man's inability to face himself. Thus the first step in the dialectic of regression was to discover the absolute irreducibility of individual fears and desires: it was impossible to gaze on death since it provoked the pure terror of 'I shall die'.[11]

The testimony of the grave was that such terror came with the human realisation of individual mortality: good reason Morin declared to use the term 'archaic' not 'primitive' for the earliest human cultures since they already grasped the human predicament.[12]

The regressive movement into the archaic psyche uncovered three connected responses: (i) The realistic awareness that death was inescapable; (ii) the trauma when the inevitable could not be accepted; (iii) the mythological solution of (i) and (ii), namely, the belief in individual survival beyond death.

The interconnection of these three responses was 'the death trauma'. The belief in immortality combined human realism since man – unlike the animal – could envisage death, with the absolute need which such knowledge encountered.[13]

From the concept of death trauma Morin developed a Freudo-Marxism in which he used Freud to expose Marxism's surrender of its commitment to satisfy need while Marx would triumphantly rebut Freud's despairing realism. Such triümph required a revision of Freud's theory on the emergence of human personality so that, for Morin, the unconscious would be captured by the force of a liberated society.

With Freud Morin saw individual consciousness and awareness of death arise together both phylogenetically (in archaic humanity) and ontogenetically (in infancy).[14] Morin endorsed Freud's declaration that each individual believed himself immortal but added that this belief proceeded from animal blindness to death so that the immortality wish was actually the assumption of amortality.[15] Freudian theory, thus reworked, supported amortality as a need. The strength of amortality as need was enhanced by Morin's revision of the Oedipus complex. Whereas Freudian orthodoxy made the death thought a consequence of the Oedipus complex, Morin proposed a common origin for death trauma and sexual repression. So the fear of death was not merely the wage of repressed sexual desire but integral to the trauma of recognising individuality: the researches of Piaget demonstrated that the child recognised simultaneously 'I am' and 'I am mortal' just as the grave proved the trauma existed in archaic humanity.[16] The complementarity of death trauma and sexual repression had already been recognised in myth and no myth had seen this more profoundly than the Christian story of original sin.[17] Christianity not only deepened Freud's insight that amortality was an absolute need; it helped Morin expand the arena of the unconscious from which revolutionary energy would be directed towards satisfying the need for amortality.

Morin expanded the Freudian unconscious so that it could mingle both animal blindness to death[18] and human traumatised repudiation of death.[19] This vast unconscious was permeated by Pascal's perception of the human predicament as a *moi* which seeks escape from fear in 'distraction', that is forgetfulness of self.

Linguistically Morin's 'coup' exploited the peculiarities of Freudian terminology in French. In French Freud's *Das Es* (the id) can be translated either as *Le Soi* (the self) or *Le ça* (the id). Morin used *Le Soi,* so identifying it with the full range of animal drives. But, he argued, the unconscious is greater than the self since it included the Ego's (*Das Ich*) inability to live with its traumas.

The French translation of *Das Ich* as *Le Moi,* the reflexive pronoun 'myself', eased Morin's insertion of Pascal's self which refuses to see itself, into the unconscious.

Morin enlisted Pascal to repudiate Marxism's narrow focus on modern bourgeois life as a unique source of alienation and yet to anticipate a Marxist triumph over distraction. If daily life with its habits and activities seemed hardly affected by the death trauma this was because human society treated death as a distraction from social life,[20] just as if it were an animal species indifferent to the life of its individual members. But society was not only indifferent, it would also strive to appropriate the death trauma 'for itself'. Just as the realisation of the inevitability of death was an individual acquisition of a socially produced knowledge, so the afterlife was conceived, produced and even allocated by human society. Marx had glimpsed the real extent of man's ambition to humanise death when, with Feuerbach, he proclaimed religion to be the realisation of the human essence as a fantasy. But the politicised culture of class struggle crowded out the insight and shrank religion into the opium of the masses.

## *Production of the Afterlife*

While human society was the author and producer of the afterlife, Morin did not waver in Marxism's materialist certainty that the afterlife thereby produced was a fantasy; in Hegelian terms it was nevertheless material since it responded to an inescapable need. Moreover materiality, in this sense, would be made more acute by the reciprocal relationship between the complexification of society and the growing autonomy of the individual not only in this, the 'real', life, but in the fantasy of afterlife.

The history of such an illusion would therefore show the extent to which magic, religion and philosophy articulated the real life of humanity. At the end of Morin's journey through the spirit world he would discover that inadapted humanity had reached crisis point since society was no longer able to cater for the needs of the individual.

Archaic humanity experienced trauma but not crisis since the individual only 'survived' as the member of a society which enveloped him after as before death. The individual was both less and other than himself: existing only as a member of society he survived only as a double, that is, a stranger lodged within the self. This stranger was *ego alter* in contrast to an *alter ego* since this latter expressed the multiplicity of the self.[21]

Ontogenetically the double persisted in the first stage of childhood awareness as indicated by the 'mirror stage' of 'Doctor Jacques

Lacan' (not yet the icon 'Lacan').[22] But as the bonds of individual to society loosened, the double broke up: one part ascended to divinity, the other made a re-entry as the soul, the double realised inside the self. The soul could thus take the identity of the individual, his Ego. Such an advance in realism had to sharpen the traumatised appetite for immortality; the most materialist response to the need for immortality came from Christianity.[23]

The Marxist truism that early Christianity had been a harbinger of socialism became for Morin a key to analysing class relationships in terms of the death trauma.

Rather than analyse the Christian apocalypse as a revolution deflected by the blockages of Roman capitalism Morin's perspective emphasised the urgency of need. The point of the crisis was the one which had needled St Paul, namely the sting of death. From the standpoint of need, Christianity expressed not an opium but recognition of a real crisis, namely that antique society could no longer restrain the anguish of death.

So the demand for immortality, far from deflecting the class conflict, expressed what the lower classes most wanted. When in archaic societies the symbiotic couple of priest–king arrogated to themselves the choicest morsels of immortality, they necessarily forbad the slave the idle dream of owning immortal subjectivity.[24] But the slave did presume to think of death and so posed a challenge: how can the fullness of immortality be democratised and realised?

The only answer Marxism gave came indirectly through Alexandre Kojève's interpretation of a section of Hegel's phenomenology, the dialectic of master and slave. In Kojève's commentary, labour instigated the materialistic optimism which could translate all desire into need. Morin's reading allowed the master–slave dialectic to be the historical account of the transition from barbarism to culture but criticised Kojève for eluding the problem of death. Morin would launch his myth of amortality from his attack on Kojève's enterprise.[25]

Through Kojève's eyes the 'master–slave' was a phenomenology of class conflict which promised its end. It began with the encounter of two conscious beings neither yet capable of recognising awareness in the other. The struggle to win recognition was a struggle of life and death in which each measured commitment to self by the readiness to die for its sake. The outcome could not be death but submission of one contestant (historically slavery). The victor in the contest, the master, thereby entered into the fullness of life. He could use this subject as another object to satisfy any desire he might have – he was lord of things, as of life: the master was essential, the slave merely his tool forced to work on dead nature which also overwhelmed him as the fear of death he had failed to overcome.

But the labour he experienced as a wage of fear held forth redemptive promise: in transforming nature, he would recover the freedom he lost: indeed the master trapped in the evanescence of desire must recognise the slave's humanity or become inessential. Labour thus was the rite of passage whereby all mankind could accede to the fullness of desire (rewritten by Marx as need) and cancel out the fear of death.[26]

Morin's reading of the master–slave dialectic exposed the limit of its Enlightenment optimism. If consciousness, accepting death, overcame the finitude of individual life and opened itself to the life of the human species, such a dialectical negation, Morin emphasised, could only take place as the act of consciousness: real biological death was not the dialectical but merely the abstract opposite of living consciousness.[27]

Hegel's idealistic 'suppression' of death consciousness had to fail if adopted by a materialistic philosophy. And yet Marx's one reference to death only made sense as a gloss on Hegel's phenomenology, seemingly unaware that such Hegelian idealism could not transpose directly into a materialistic reversal of Hegel's dialectic since, in reality, the event remained untouched. The master–slave dialectic is not a struggle to the death but a struggle in which death is risked. 'The being which has risked death and lived can live humanely', Hegel had stated. 'The risk of death only makes sense for the one who does not die', Morin commented.[28] Historically the master–slave dialectic expressed the conflict between barbarism (the master) and culture (the slave transformed by labour). Such deflation exposed the blind spots of idealist dialectic. For the master wanted immortality, not simply to enjoy his ownership of the other. Barbarism, Morin pointed out, is charged with killing, a desire to exterminate derived from the master's horrified helplessness before biological death. Indeed the more consciousness or ideology designated the master to be 'God's double' the more intensely did this god's other body feel the terror of mortality. Writing in 1950 Morin could say explicitly what Hegel glimpsed when he said negation was 'liberty, otherwise crime'. The master's power over death was merely to inflict it on as many slaves as he could – so Nero or the SS could elaborate a science of death agonies.[29] But, we can ask, if Hegel was almost unconscious of the real depth of barbarism, did not Marxism, idealistically, share Hegel's myopia as to the common root of slavery and murder, the 'rational' and the 'irrational' uses of mastery?

Marx had inherited Hegel's vision of civilised consciousness.[30] But, Morin warned, culture and barbarism were symbiotic antagonists.[31] And even the risk of death could disguise itself as its opposite as with: 'The silent ones who avoid the risk of death to let their thoughts live.'[32]

Marx's dependence on Hegel induced objections. In terms of political ideologies Morin made a strong critique of Marxist inability to admit the irrationality of fascism (barbarism).

Philosophically the risk of death legitimated the revolutionary socialist enterprise. But since Hegel's phenomenology had lost its idealistic claim to merge the human individual with the purpose or destiny of his species, Marxism could not rely on Hegel to vindicate its utopian horizons.

Marxism might elude these problems but their effects permeated Morin's characterisation of the 'contemporary crisis of death'. The crisis intensified the failure of Marx to resolve the death trauma. Morin therefore invoked the energy of Marxism to solve its own 'distraction'.

### *The Crisis*

Morin's perception of the socio-historical character of the crisis – that of the isolated bourgeois individual – belonged to the truisms of Marxist analysis. Many of Marxism's illustrious names, Lukacs especially, held that bourgeois irrationalism stemmed from the bourgeoisie's artificial longevity.[33]

The dialectic of adaptation–inadaptation charged these truisms with a divergent significance. The neuroses, the nihilism, the exaltation of the animal self, the search for supermen, and the transformation of life into a game might all be traced to the collapse of societal order and the isolation of individual consciousness. But the inadaptation of the bourgeois individual to his individuality was permeated by 'distractions': class conflict and social roles in this perspective were conduits for a trauma in eruption. Thus the crisis of bourgeois individualism was not primarily one of bourgeois irrationality.

For a communist to set Heidegger and Sartre as the negative and positive poles of existentialism was a bold enterprise: bolder still was Morin's willingness to legitimate the sense of their projects, namely to gaze on death and yet live authentically. Heidegger fell short of the authenticity he demanded, since living with death became for him an ecstasy which, born from anguish, nevertheless became its magical transfiguration, forgetting that: 'Anguish itself reveals to us that death and nothingness are opposed to our most profound being.'[34]

But what Heidegger forgot in existentialism, Marxism forgot in revolutionary ecstasy. The crisis, as seen by Morin, was one where the left hand of Hegel (revolutionary universalism) had lost all contact with the right hand (the individual's ability to accept his destiny).

> Today revolutionary philosophies put death into parentheses and the philosophies of reaction place themselves beneath the sign of death. But this does not mean that all philosophies which put death into parentheses are revolutionary nor that all those obsessed by death are reactionaries.[35]

It led to the same conclusion Freud had reached: 'We cannot keep our old attitude to death and have not found a new one yet.'[36]

## *Prometheus Storms Nirvana*

A scheme for the scientific conquest of death might be appropriately proposed by one who was a voracious consumer of science fiction. Dating from 1950 Morin's prediction has the air of a time machine from a film when the passerby steps into a gallery of discarded instruments. Only three years later Crick and Watson discovered the DNA structure which controls all living organisms and early in the same year Stalin died, although, as Morin said: 'We had ended by thinking him immortal.'[37]

For this reason I set aside the details of Morin's science; its central thrust was an optimism held by some biologists founded on experiments which demonstrated that unicellular bacteria reproduced by the division of the original cell;[38] they left no corpse and in that sense offered a model of 'amortality'. Neither the evidence nor the optimism which fed off the evidence were specifically Marxist but rather reconnected Marxism to the Enlightenment's scientism (faith in science). Thus when Morin invoked science as 'praxis, namely knowledge and action', he was echoing Metalnikov, a Russian liberal émigré from the Bolshevik Revolution, whose *The Struggle Against Death* gave Morin the title of his concluding chapter.[39] Such super-optimism fitted Morin's stance as a heretic of the era of Stalin, around whose 'indestructible' person communism had built a culture which claimed the power to overturn natural obstacles for proletarian science.

The most notorious instance where this ideology led to a breach between Soviet and non-Soviet scientists was the claim of the Soviet biologist Lysenko to have produced cereals with characteristics learnt from its parent seed. Morin was already a dissident when Lysenkoism became mandatory for communist propaganda in 1948.[40] But while Morin ignored 'proletarian science' and its proto-Maoist belief that politics could command science he was touched by its triumphalist culture.

Morin as a heretic could express the mythic drive of the Enlightenment's scientism. The distinction between the amortality of unicellular life and the mortality of sexual life confirmed the Christian intuition which connected sexuality with death as well as Freud's speculations in which Eros, the life instinct, and Thanatos, the death instinct, were inseparable combatants. The possibility that death and sex were only opportunist evolutionary devices had already induced Metalnikov to call for an 'international organisation for the struggle against death'.[41]

The call echoed in *L'Homme* would stay with Morin even when he ceased to believe that its 'science' was feasible: in California in 1969 he noted just such an organisation, product of the American 'New Age'.[42]

The programme could thus combine science, myth and philosophy. The Hegelian merging between the individual and species would be materialised by instalments: the extensions of lifespan by specific numbers of years moved towards an indefinite extension of life. This indefinite boundary would give the material man the same life expectation as the double of archaic human fantasy. But it would be fully human, for unlike the double or the unicellular amoeba it had been 'enriched by the experience of death'.[43] I comment, paraphrasing Hegel, 'Only he who has risked death and lives indefinitely can live humanely.'

My reformulation indicates the two joints through which the religious status of the myth glared forth. Morin deliberately evaded answering two questions where any response would expose the degree to which he had turned Marxism into a negative theology. One question concerns the sort of being who might extract the profit of the promise of amortality: would such a being still be human? The other and complementary question is what sort of barrier would persist or arise between amortality and immortality.

The first requires a speculative futurology and therefore escapes any specific answer: Morin could therefore cite the Marxist texts which proclaimed a radical break between actual and future humanity while providing no details of this transformation. To the second question Morin could give some response if only through a glass darkly: amortality did not cancel death. To begin with not for the dead – Mayakovsky's ringing call to future scientists, 'Resurrect me first, I so loved life',[44] would never be answered. But then was death cancelled for the amortals? For even were they to 'domesticate' and 'colonise' their own species life, they would escape the tyranny of species reproduction only to face the ultimate death of all, that of the Cosmos.[45]

In the presence of cosmic death the distinction between amortality and immortality melted, for Morin, into a grandiose continuum. If biological death was 'stupid as a cabbage'[46] human finitude was raised to the infinity of the universe as it gazed on its last moments.

In this continuum the Hegelian concept of the good infinite could at last be realised. Into it Morin poured Marx's intuitive vision that fully materialised man would in fact no longer be 'man', and speculated that death itself would no longer be death through the physical transformation of human biology. The absence of any real answer to our first question emboldened Morin to envisage amortal beings who could materialise the cosmic mythologies which humanity had accumulated.

In a blaze of enthusiasm Morin made Hegel a bridge into the infinity of the universe.

> Individual amortality would lead to the search for a totality, a loving fusion with the world in which it would also negate itself. For if individual affirmation is a fundamental human tendency, cosmic participation is the second.
>
> We can suppose that minds ... capable of dislocation, will unite in a dialectic of love where they will lose their individuality and impregnate the cosmos ... And so in this hypothesis where the ship of man, navigator of time and space, embarks towards infinite night the dialectic of the transcendence of individuality would move towards a cosmic fulfilment of a positive Nirvana.[47]

The invocation of Nirvana merged all the discrepancies of this Marxist myth which both fulfilled the Hegelian legacy and criticised its Prometheanism. For the mode of entry into Nirvana was appropriate to the cosmic materialism of Marx's contemporary, Richard Wagner. Morin's vision of cosmic death resonated with the entry into Valhalla and the subsequent magnificence of the *Götterdämmerung*.

Such a sensualist, possibly erotic, extreme to which Morin willed the Prometheus myth of Marxism, carried the seeds of its own extinction. 'Prometheus' indeed disappeared in Morin's conversion experience of 1969 as if he had been Morin's Marxist double. But the need for cosmic unity will reappear in *La Méthode*, only this time as the tragic fraternity of unredeemed humanity.

CHAPTER 4

# The End of Marxist Fellowship

In 1956, having broken his isolation, Morin embarked on the quest for fellowship in Marxism. In 1968 the glow of socialist brotherhood faded from his life. An adventure which began with the excitement of Khrushchev's destalinisation and the Hungarian revolution ended in the false spring of May 1968. But in Morin's inner life the adventure had really ended in 1962, when he chose to scuttle *Arguments*. In his subsequent ideological alliance with Lefort and Castoriadis, 'apparatus communism' loomed increasingly large as the major obstacle in the way of a self-regulating socialism. Morin swiftly activated his hopes in response to the events of May 1968; he was among the first intellectuals to proclaim that a revolutionary carnival had begun. But the publication of his articles together with those of Lefort and Castoriadis (writing under his fourth pseudonym Coudray) marked the exhaustion of their joint project. The discrepancies between the allies revealed that this was a shadow alliance operational only in its hostility to Marxist totalitarianism.

The decisive moment in this story was that of an intellectual and personal crisis which Morin built around the collapse of *Arguments*. Morin's final solution would only begin to emerge from his year in California. This chapter argues that the collapse of *Arguments* not only plunged Morin into another crisis but revealed to him that crisis was his vocation.

## *The Orchestrator*

*Arguments* was founded in an anti-chauvinist spirit by being twinned with the journal of Italian communist dissidents, *Raggionamenti.*[1] Its official founders were Morin, Duvignaud, Pierre Fougeyrollas, Henri Lefebvre and Barthes.

By the time of its 'gentle suicide' it had drawn contributions from almost all the leading names of the non-communist Left in France with two significant exceptions: Castoriadis and Sartre. It also published previously unavailable foreign works, notably of all the Frankfurt school and extracts from Lukacs' *History and Class Consciousness,* which drew an angry letter from the old Lukacs, by then a respectable communist in Budapest.

If *Arguments'* core concerns were those of the philosophies, movements and institutions connected to Marxism the issues and articles also ranged through the politics and sociology of modern France, the Western world and the Third World. It devoted several issues to psychoanalysis, the modernisation of Eros, biology, physics and scientific speculation. Eventually Nietzsche and Heidegger would loom as large as Marx in its philosophic interrogations. At the time of its 'gentle suicide' the following issues were among those announced only to be unborn:

Technics and civilisation.
Language.
The Sacred.
Money.
Dictionary of Leftist myth.
Adventure.
Art and the Dwelling.

Throughout its existence Morin was the most prolific contributor, followed by Axelos, who joined in 1957, and by Duvignaud. No one else got into double figures, although Fougeyrollas, Fejto, the psychoanalyst Gabel, psychosociologist Lapassade, and sociologists Touraine and Naville, were deeply involved. Barthes drifted in and out; Lefebvre would incite hostility to the enterprise once he realised that its open Marxism involved the likelihood of shooting past Marxism. Mascolo could stomach the spiritual and intellectual anarchy of the journal even less than Lefebvre. *Arguments'* desire to float freely was, I suggest, why Castoriadis could not contribute and why Sartre's *Les Temps Modernes* was almost as much 'the enemy' as was the PCF.

*Arguments'* impact on French Marxism can be visualised through the metaphor of a city in insurrection (Budapest physically, Paris intellectually). There was a barricade, with the PCF and its supporter *Les Temps Modernes* on one side, *Arguments* and *Socialisme ou barbarie* (*SB*) on the other. The issue on the barricade was whether the Hungarian insurrection was merely a setback for the communist world or, as *Arguments* would have it, the beginning of its end. Thus the PCF could allow its increasingly existentialist philosopher Garaudy to debate with Sartre, but not with *Arguments*. Conversely *Arguments* was drawn to *SB*, although the spirit of a Marxism of questions not answers was as foreign to *SB* as to the PCF. Morin, as the great enthusiast for an 'interrogative Marxism', was not only the spiritual founder of *Arguments* but emblem or standard-bearer of the insurrection.

For Morin the brotherhood of *Arguments* was personal, political and philosophic.[2] Within the PCF, authentic comradeship was a shameful secret. Now the 'we could not accept' of dissidence could become the 'we can disagree' of political debate. Such a 'we' engendered a philosophic direction.

In the debates on the status of Marxism Morin set out to limit its claims and open its intellectual frontiers. He argued for a Marxism which would not limit philosophy by being either its end or its cancellation, but primarily a praxis directing political action. What he sought from *Arguments* was to demonstrate how action in this sense was inseparable from individual commitment and debate free from the fear of being on trial. More than any other contributor he projected his persona the 'I, Edgar Morin' in all issues so as to confirm the intellectual by the personal. Hence his recurrent analyses of the *Arguments* group were, for him, not only a 'sociology of the group' but a vital element of intellectual sanity. Hence also the 'house style' under which *Arguments* was launched and for which it became famous (in Paris).

Not only did *Arguments* not issue an ideological manifesto, as did the generality of Parisian intellectual journals, it also claimed to be not a journal but a research bulletin.[3] The initial issues of *Arguments* read like discussions held after lunch: a statement or thesis (in deference to the phantom of Marx) attracted responses and replies in bursts of about a page. Unfriendly critics compared *Arguments*' dinners to the *agapes* (friendship feasts) of the primitive church. The close relationship with *Raggionamenti* fostered a glow of international brotherhood.

While Duvignaud and Axelos followed Morin in the quantity of contributed pages, their relationship with Morin expressed the hopes, tensions and collapse of his project.

Duvignaud was Morin's indispensable interlocutor, so that we could say the proposition 'Morin created *Arguments*' and 'Morin with Duvignaud created the fellowship of *Arguments*' are both true. They were an existential nuclear couple acting out the mode of interrogation through the roles of believer and doubter, with Morin the optimist and Duvignaud the grumbler. When Morin wrote 'All goes well', Duvignaud would reply (as we shall see), 'All goes well, but'.

Axelos's growing presence induced a watershed in 1959, the year he replaced Morin as editor-in-chief (but not as principal contributor nor animator). With Axelos as editor, the format and title became definitively that of a journal,[4] with contributors organised around, rather than debating, a major theme. Axelos himself was given to gnomic aphorisms and philosophic fables. Being Heideggerean, and hence cosmically relaxed about humanising Marxism – unlike Morin or Duvignaud – he seemed to interrogate not others but either himself, Heidegger or God.

One need not metamorphose Axelos into a Heideggerean serpent in a Marxist garden, but his presence and editorial strategy would augment the ambiguity of the legend of *Arguments* and becloud

Morin's seminal inspiration. Morin's role was further obscured by the shadowy afterlife of *Arguments,* namely the series of books published under the rubric *Collection Arguments*, after the 'suicide' of the journal. The collection, necessarily far removed from Morin's intended praxis for *Arguments,* was a symptom of the end he feared.

### *The Moral Autonomy of Arguments*

*Arguments* operated by constantly checking its pulse. In 1959 Duvignaud asked whether anything solid existed in the flow of communal discussion. The real lives of the group, he suggested, had ended back in 1944 (Morin's euphoria) when the Resistance failed to become a revolution. Now their alternatives were either empty revisionist theology or academic specialisation. Either the team became adults or they would become the 'bourgeoisie of radicalism'.[5]

Morin took up Duvignaud's challenge as an opportunity to found an 'auto-éthique', an ethics of autonomy and self-examination which could serve the *Arguments* team as a lode star. In 'What is to be Done?', an ironic reference to Lenin's pamphlet, he characterised *Arguments* as the other side of the communist drive for identity through unity: 'We seek no sect, school or spiritual family and remain a group of comrades free in our mutual criticisms.'[(6)]

To avoid becoming Duvignaud's 'defrocked revolutionaries' required not self-effacement but self-examination. The process of self-examination became central to Morin's entries in the debate on the philosophic status of Marxism since this would involve the crisis of the Marxist belief in 'total man', which he had indirectly challenged in *L'Homme.*

### *Meta-Marxism*

The debates on Marxism as philosophy were provoked by Axelos and Duvignaud. Axelos, with Heideggerian nihilism, proposed a rebirth of philosophy from the death of all philosophies, including that of Marx;[7] Duvignaud was more concerned to free the proletariat from the ideological confines into which Marxism had restricted it.[8] Morin channelled Axelos's aphorisms 'describing' an infinitely open worldliness and Duvignaud's demands for general revision of Marxism into a critique of 'total man' in which nevertheless the utopian themes were retained. The critique of Marxism as a philosophy of 'Total Man' seemed, during the phase of *Arguments,* almost to reinforce Morin's attachment to its Hegelian residues of myth and science fiction, shielding them from Axelos's cosmic nihilism.

Morin used a cultural metaphor to connect the fragmentation of 'total man' to his optimistic belief in salvaging the Marxist enterprise. Marx, he said, was part Einstein.[9] He had achieved the equivalent of Einstein's 'special relativity theory' but not his 'general relativity theory'. Marx's 'special relativity theory' was to perceive the mutual conditioning of natural and human history when, as in the 1844 manuscripts, he predicted that 'the natural sciences will enfold the science of man and the science of man enfold the natural sciences.' Marx, however, had not been able to grasp the relativity of time even in its sense of progression in history; he had not come to terms with the mythical character of reality. Morin thus demanded both a realisation of all that was myth in Marxism and the centrality of myth to human beings. 'General relativity' would commit humans to living in contradiction.

'Total man' was so inwardly fractured as to fragment under scrutiny. The concept of alienation had to be released from its ideological employment as a critique of the inadequacies of bourgeois or socialist societies and turned on itself; the recognition that the concept of alienation was itself alienated stemmed from the recognition that total man (or Marx man) was himself an alienated ideal: rupture and contradiction were, as Pascal, Kierkegaard and Nietzsche all insisted, fundamental to all human experience.[10]

Morin was hit by a disabused revelation. How could it have taken so long to see that 'total man', reconciled with his own nature and Nature, was a religious myth?[11]

But if Morin could share Axelos's vision of the crack-up of 'total man' his instinctual response was Hegelian, not Heideggerian. The power of myth filled him with a sense of the fullness of the void even if that sense rested on illusion. Moreover, Morin could retain a commitment to science in which the mythology of *L'Homme* would be more real than reality and certainly more real than Marxism.[12]

The power of such myth transpired in the 'science fiction' futurism Morin encouraged at *Arguments*. Here Morin reworked the utopianism of need he had explored in *L'Homme*.

Several issues of *Arguments* addressed the speculative implications of science, technology and fiction. Against the disdainful anti-scientism of Sartre's *Les Temps Modernes*, *Arguments* encouraged speculation on science as a matter of mental hygiene.

In September 1958 *Arguments* organised a party game in the form of a 'questionnaire on anticipation'. Of the thirteen questions three seem to drop straight from *L'Homme*, namely:

> Can death be suppressed?
> What are the limits of Science?
> Can you imagine the future of the world? – Disintegration, eternal return (a reference to Nietzsche)

While other questions, such as mutation of the species, anticipated Morin's subsequent concerns, he and Axelos alone entered fully the spirit of the game. Most contributors abstained; Duvignaud answered sceptically. To the question 'Can death be suppressed?' Morin's answer was more categorical than in 1951: 'Amortality can be achieved ... the death of humanity will be that of the cosmos.'[13]

Freed from the constraint of Party membership, Morin could predict that science was poised to fulfil needs which previously myth had satisfied magically.

Restoration of youth, telecommunication either by being one's own double (so virtual reality fulfils the magical dream of bilocation) or metamorphosis were all on the agenda.

In the flood tide of cosmological optimism Morin could suggest that even these new contradictions would yield. If the cosmos seemed promised for self-destruction: 'The force of intelligence of which we know but the human aspect, seems engaged in a struggle against disintegration',[14] he wrote, echoing Freud's depiction of Eros setting out yet again in battle against Death.

Cosmic optimism coloured Morin's vision of the planetary era, but this vision now turned against the communism which had first inspired it.

Speculating about the twenty-first century, Morin declared that the twentieth had been that of state socialism, that is of Leninist regimes. Endorsing a belief widespread in the late 1950s, Morin envisaged a convergence between state socialism and its state capitalist rival, drawn together by the unification which would characterise the planetary era. But the convergence could either work through the bureaucratic structures common to the rivals or the federative, libertarian form of true socialism.

The prediction that the twenty-first century would see a 'socialism against the state' had to do not with historical determinism but the mythic realism Morin believed to be at the heart of Marxism.[15]

So in order to relaunch the message and the myth of Marxism whilst its systematic coherence was foundering, Morin reintroduced ethical concerns into the praxis which alone was worth rescuing. Characteristically, in *Arguments 7*, devoted to the dialectic, Axelos's contribution was 'Dialectic and Philosophy', Morin's 'Dialectic and Politics'.[16]

Marx and Hegel, Morin reminded his comrades, had derided 'it must be' as an immature, religious premonition of 'it will be done'. In a negative sense Lukacs rightly claimed that to search for moral renewal was the subjective side of the absence of totality. So to embark on such a search was finally to relinquish the claim to self-sufficience of 'it will be done' and a way of salvaging praxis from its wreck. But once the power of imagination was recognised, the ethical significance of political action could not be dismissed.

Marxist realism had bankrupted itself in failing to detect that the real was permeated by the imaginary.

If revolutionary action was to work through fragmented totality it would have to make imagination its guide, but such imagination must itself be nourished by the complexity of the real; it must avoid letting action become a pretext to divide the world into good and evil (as Stalin did) or, like Sartre, bet all on a single project.

But at least in 1958 Morin still 'knew' how the project should appear: he could draw on the Hungarian uprising as an instance of a revolutionary movement drawing strength from a multiplicity of forces, parties and individual responses. By 1962, the hopes of a multifaceted but revolutionary commitment had faded and with them the rationale of *Arguments*. Just before the 'gentle suicide' Morin and Lapassade produced an article on microsocial socialism, capable of meeting non-revolutionary as well as revolutionary contexts.[17]

From the variety, virtually a shopping list, of communalist experiments, of workers' councils and Anarcho-Syndicalist groupings, Morin and Lapassade discerned a rift between the political as politics of 'the Party' and the politics of human relationships. The energies of the intelligentsia they suggested should be channelled far more towards the politics of interpersonal relationships. The failures of microsocial paths to socialism in the past they suggested had been fuelled by their lack of attention to the social problems of daily life, especially in the workplace. Hence intellectuals could intervene in the detection as well as responses to relationships within groups in such a way as to facilitate the ultimate objective of self-governing communities. Noting the alarm sounded by Herbert Marcuse that technical intellectuals such as psycho-sociologists functioned as 'eliminators of conflict' (In *One Dimensional Man* capitalism is the ultimate brainwashing system and psychoanalysts its ultimate brainwashers), the article suggested they might rather prove 'illuminators of contradictions'.

The divergent destinies of Lapassade and Morin neatly illustrate the ambiguity of their joint article.[18] Lapassade emerged as an organiser in the spontaneous insurgency of May 1968 whereas Morin was vacating not only the party political but any political activism. His sociological writings offered the first sympathetic French response to mass culture. In *Present Time* he placed the atomisation of the individual in the global context of a culture in fertile evolution: this new mythology turned human time into a continual present of self-gratification and thereby liberated personal life from the burdens of state, class or religion. *Present Time* enlarged the theme of *Cinéma* that the actors on screen transmuted the archaic double into the eternal present of modern technology. Morin's interventionist sociology of *Report from a French Village* and *Rumour in*

*Orleans* would address the multiplying conflicts of the late 1960s as tensions generated by the modernisation of French society rather than issues of class. Morin was especially drawn to the power of archaic myths and religious beliefs to reorganise and reactivate themselves as exemplified by the rumour in Orleans about white women sold into Arab slavery. Morin's focus on the imaginary relates to the third debate, the dialogue with 'Trotskyism' but more especially *Socialisme ou barbarie (SB)* about the nature of power.

### *Apparatus Communism*

The search to understand the Soviet state and system was not only *Arguments*' leading intellectual endeavour but would colour most of its analyses of social and political theories. The questions 'what is a class?', 'what is a 'bureaucracy', and 'what is state power?' were either generated by reflections on the Soviet system or would at some stage in most articles lead to considerations on how communist regimes operated. Morin used these debates to launch the expression 'apparatus communism': the expression 'apparatus' would remain central to his analytic vocabulary, although its significance would be enlarged with *La Méthode*. Now both Morin's analysis and his relationship to language indicated how *SB* formed an odd couple with *Arguments*. The analysis *SB* introduced, through Lefort, into the pages of *Arguments* had its roots in its rivalry with more orthodox Trotskyists such as Naville who also entered the debate in the pages of *Arguments*. Unlike Naville, for whom the Soviet bureaucracy was merely a stratum encrusted onto the proletariat in an imperfectly socialist regime, Lefort analysed the bureaucracy as a class ruling over a regime of bureaucratic capitalism. In contrast to all other varieties of Trotskyism *SB* saw the bureaucratic capitalism of the Soviet regime not as a pale reflection of other capitalist systems but as the highest and most dangerous stage of modern capitalism.[19]

Morin responded with sympathetic interest but nevertheless he sensed that here was a word-magic reminiscent of the one imposed by the communist party. To focus on the distinction between bureaucracy as stratum or as class abstracted the Soviet regime into a magic world of names; it missed out both the institutional and human aspects of how power actually operated. Here Morin began to sketch out a perspective, that of apparatus, as a way of explaining the dynamics of power. The word apparatus would undergo a great transformation after 1970. Nevertheless his final thoughts on the Soviet apparatus (see chapter 9) were already present in this debate.

Morin's impatience with Lefort's label-juggling reached back to his experience (in prefaces to the re-edition of *Autocritique* he proclaimed it an analysis of apparatus communism).[20] Words such as proletariat and class seemed obscure. The only entity whose existence was certain was the 'unique–monolithic–party–of–the–proletariat'. To grasp how its power operated required not a theology of class but a perception of the extraordinary dynamism of the system. The essential contrast has to be found within the apparatus between the elements promoting dynamism (the *apparatchiks*) and the bureaucrats maintaining stability. 'The *apparatchik* is active, the bureaucrat passive'.[21] But this formula could not encompass a highly complex phenomenon. The Stalinist party condensed a dynamic relationship between apparatuses of decision-making, technicians responsible for industrialisation and a bureaucracy largely charged with the execution of decisions taken outside its sphere into an open-caste system where not only the personnel but the existence of specific castes was highly fluid. The only fixed point was Stalin, the supreme apparatus.[22] A somewhat angry Lefort replied to denounce the 'demonology of power' in Morin's concept of apparatus.[23] Such a response exposed the absence of common ground: in Lefort's class-struggle perspective the bureaucracy was clearly visible as a machinery of exploitation while issues of science and technology seemed almost invisible. The socialisation of labour, Lefort declared, had exploded the functions of management. Consequently the managerial class only had a negative function: it prevented full proletarian socialised labour.

Morin's exchange with Lefort characterised not only the place of *Arguments* on the French Left but of Morin in *Arguments*. As he said, he was tainted by 'scientism' even in a team which wanted to break away from the prevalent assumption that science and technology had nothing new to say about the essentials of the class struggle.[24] So when Lefort and Castoriadis threw overboard their Marxist ballast they could share with Morin an ideological alliance based on themes of social self-regulation and anti-totalitarianism. But Morin would remain unique in the search to ground self-regulation in the processes of physics and biology, a mark possibly of his 'failure' to complete the humanist curriculum of French academic training.

## *The Permanent Crisis*

The decision to close *Arguments* was taken collectively; Morin, Axelos and Duvignaud all wrote a valedictory article.[25] But, if Axelos said farewell with the passing sorrow of a wanderer, Morin burst into a lament for a lost love. Indeed Morin experienced the end of *Arguments* not as a beginning but as an intellectual and personal crisis. The crisis became manifest in *Le Vif* (1969), *Politique* (1965) and *Mai '68*.

*Le Vif*, published last, was actually the first to be written, since it was the record of Morin's crisis of the years 1962–3. In his 1968 'post preface' he wrote: 'My other books came from me. This is myself.'[26]

Formally the book is a diary; it records the history of a medical collapse with the promise of a fruitful recovery. The physical collapse might have been psychosomatic, but required long hospitalisation at the Mount Sinai Jewish Hospital in New York (a glut of symbols). But the diary (surely intended for publication) tells the reader that the Ego of Edgar Morin had been presiding over the disintegration of his marriage, his sexual stability and, with *Arguments*, of his public voice. It was the first and richest of several books by Morin which were books about writing a book. Precisely for this reason it stamped Morin as an outsider in French culture in an age when the dominant literary quest was for books which either dispensed with or hid their author. Far from the jaded sexual titillation of the author who simulates self-exclusion in his text, Morin made himself extravagantly if not indecently naked. To be sure the nakedness was justified by his crisis, but the crisis itself involved Morin declaring himself a man who lived in and (who knows?) for crisis.

From this barely structured kaleidoscope of musings, imagined and real arguments and ideas, some furtive, others turned into projects which dissolve into each other, I elicit a clash between the private and the public Edgar Morin. First, we can note that this was a metamorphosis of *Autocritique*. There the 'real Edgar Morin' had emerged from the politically motivated suppression of personality demanded by a public body, the PCF. But this time the conflict of public and private personas stemmed entirely from Morin as in all his subsequent autobiographies. Secondly, we can note with Morin that the cacophony of ideas represented a mass of issues he was in the process of digesting. *Le Vif* anticipated *La Méthode* by virtue of the questions posed but not the answers provided. I therefore bypass the wealth of schemas to depict the crisis intellectually as a question of communication. So far, Morin confided, he had worked on 'medium-wave', that is, he had accepted empiricist rationalism and had addressed the issues of 'anthropology-history-sociology-politics'.[27]

On other frequencies, however, he received messages which were inaudible on medium-wave. The medium-wave excluded messages of mystery, miracle, revelation, dreams, of the ecstasies of losing oneself in sex, as well as the sense of becoming oneself.

Such messages on medium-wave could only be heard as illusion, and yet Morin was seized with the feeling that illusion for him was more real than reality. In print, we recall, Morin had proclaimed that science would solve any disturbances to the medium-wave (even those needs previously satisfied only in fantasy). But to 'the diary' Morin confided that reality itself appeared to him a sort of magic with science as a lantern projecting spectral and unresolved contradictions; they seemed not to belong to the reassuring dialectic of 'Hegelo-Marxism' but a 'savage dialectic' (years later he would give the savage dialectic the name of dialogic).[28]

One leitmotif stemmed from the work of the Lukacsian Josef Gabel: Gabel had argued that madness stemmed from a reified consciousness of reality, in particular of the flow of time.[29] But, Morin asked himself, what if reality was itself a reification?

He confided his thoughts to his lover. 'God', she replied, but Morin was 'surprised' that he had not even thought of God and yet: 'I believe in mystery, yes in mystery ... the Unknown.'[30]

And so Morin directed himself towards a search: how could he bring his own experiences of others, his intuitions about the cosmos as well as the dissolution science was inflicting on everyday reality into some sort of comprehensible contact with that reality? How could the mathematical formulas by which alone the fantastic world of physics could bear some relationship to the experienced world of the flesh, be released from a reified formalism?

### *Must We Renounce Our Nature?*

*Le Vif* was possessed by Morin's private crisis but the same feeling, less personalised, also inhabited *Politique*. In it Morin set the fragmented complexity of mankind against the assurances of his former faith.

> Marx man turns around his productive centre. Man the producer sees the consumer of pleasure, the player, the fantasist and man of myth as his alienations or derivatives.[31]

This Prometheus, illegitimate child of Hegel's spirit and bourgeois property, had no doubt his destiny was the conquest of nature. The question was however, not will there be conquest but what will be its meaning? A 'Copernican revolution' in the perception of technology occurred not only with a philosopher – Heidegger – but with Heisenberg, one of the fathers of quantum mechanics. Reversing Marx, both sensed man as instrument of a 'metabiological process' operated through technology. In the end, Morin speculated, a new, 'science fiction' being, *métanthrope* (transformed or super man), might mingle Prometheus and mutant. The revolutionary question was not simply that of fulfilment but 'must we renounce our nature?',[32] with all the difficulties such complexity posed for an 'ontological reform of man'.

In the face of such uncertainty Morin floated between several paths, unsure as to how they would integrate. Together with a

Marxism centred on production Morin reiterated his appeal to science now characterised as 'neo-scientism' to indicate that it sought not to secularise the religious aspiration to 'the truth of the world' of the old scientism (and the young Edgar Morin) but 'to question truth, matter, logic and man himself'.[33] Together with Freud (or rather with Freud's humanist interpreters such as Erich Fromm) Morin proposed a secularisation of the Christian invocation of love in a fraternity which would be both Eros and Agape.

Morin still expected those paths to meet along the satisfaction of polymorphous need; he still insisted that one day 'humanity must seriously engage amortality, its most unbelievable demand.'[34] But when it came to specifying the actors through whom these torrential demands would take shape, Morin was less certain. The decisive word in the politics of man could not come from political parties where: 'In the name of fraternity brother bites brother ... the true militants of man will not distribute tracts but will live differently.'[35]

While Morin could still appeal to a deepening of microsocial activities, there were few indications as to how the paths of neo-scientism and fraternity would effectively connect. No social class, neither the proletariat, nor the masses, nor the intellectuals, could either possess or be entrusted with such a mission. Maybe, he mused, a 'generational class, youth, might become, not the age of messiah, but the special bearer of the politics of man.'[36]

Such lines represented one of many prophecies any anthology could collect of the May student revolt. Morin's special aptitude was to grasp almost immediately that his prophecy was being materialised.

## *False Dawn in May*

On 17 May, 'immediately' after the great demonstration of the 13th, Morin burst into print in *Le Monde*, with the first of four articles collectively titled 'La Commune Étudiante'.[37] His exceptional speed into print marked his sense of the occasion and his sympathies. Nevertheless Morin was more a witness to grand history than a 'political' convert.

Morin proclaimed a youth festival, indicative of the resurgence of a primordial conflict. The student commune restored to class war its archaic meaning of a battle between generations. So, characteristically, Morin was as much the first anthropologist as well as first historian of these events. In the revolt of the sons against 'the civilisation of adult fathers' Morin discerned the recovery of a previous, presumably mythic, conflict within the species.

But what of the direction into the future? It presaged revolution but would this topple an order built on authority or would it engender new sorts of authority? Morin expressed these possibilities through the metaphor of two famous revolutionary ships. Would the commune be *Potemkin* (insubordination, revolt) or would it prove *Aurora* (the cruiser used by the Bolsheviks to seize Petrograd in 1917)? The term Commune Aurora was a distancing pun: it implied that the commune might prove a false dawn. Even the anarchists 'led' by Cohn Bendit, Morin pointed out, had no feel for liberal as opposed to libertarian values nor did they show any grasp of how apparatus communism functioned (repeating the bias of Russian anarchism of 1917–20).[38]

Morin's pun expressed a fundamental divergence between himself and his collaborators in the collected articles of *Mai '68* as well as their close ally Alain Touraine. Lefort and Castoriadis saw in the decentralised modalities of confrontation politics a breach towards a revolutionary movement for which they could proffer, if not tracts, then at least lessons, objectives, strategies and prospects.[39] Touraine was less directorial (he was not an anarchist). Nevertheless he also insisted that May 1968 had begun a new movement in need of 'revolutionary will'.[40] In the long run the fading of May 1968 enhanced Morin's claim to prescience. In the immediate aftermath Morin was already prepared to bid farewell to revolutionary Paris. That his California journey had such a meaning was clear both to Morin and to nameless detractors who called it treason.[41]

At the Salk Institute Morin further developed the project of tuning the 'medium-wave' to other frequencies. But the answers he began to find were altering rapidly.

The crisis wherein his Promethean Marxism, attached to the unquenchable power of need, clashed with biological processes working through the human species, was resolved by extinguishing Prometheus. His soundings in biology established that mortality was the inescapable consequence of cumulative accidents in the DNA programme although each failure was random. Randomness would become the problem from which *La Méthode* grew; but the entire loss of the old faith was experienced in America as liberation or as Morin wrote: 'Je suis intellectuellement high.'[42]

CHAPTER 5

# Chaosmos

*La Méthode* originated in Morin's search for principles of organisation which eventually he would term organisationalism,[1] distinguished from systems theories in general and holistic versions of systems theory by Morin's invocation of a universe permeated by the dialogic of order and disorder. His last word for such a universe is 'chaosmos'.

Chaosmos is a portmanteau neologism which packs together the words cosmos and chaos.[2] Cosmos indicates that the universe is unique or a 'singularity'. Chaos is not disorder but an implicate order resembling that proposed by the physicist David Bohm, for whom the physical categories of the universe emerge from a hidden, possibly unknown, unity of space, time and matter.[3] Chaosmos takes the shape of a circuit between the material categories of the universe and consciousness, whether human or otherwise (but most certainly not 'God'), of the universe. For Morin such a circuit engages a dialogic of order and disorder where neither is the foundation of the other. The shape of *La Méthode* expresses Morin's conviction that the universe and our knowledge of it constitute a good circle or spiral where the primacy of surface order disappears.[4] So *La Méthode* begins and ends with the relationships of order and disorder which allow the mind to constitute the universe while being constituted by it, such that the universe is both entirely 'invented' and entirely the material creator of mind. *La Méthode* is an incomplete work since two further volumes, one on evolution, the other on humanity, were promised but are as yet undelivered. Nevertheless such incompleteness fits well with Morin's concept of an open spiral: he declares at the beginning of *Idées*, its 'last' volume, that it could have been the first.[5]

In this and the next three chapters which are concerned with *La Méthode* and Morin's exposition of its issues in *Science,* I attempt to relay the sense of a spiral which is incomplete but does not require completeness. By happy 'coincidence', since *La Méthode's* recurring dramas are reminiscent of Wagner's *Ring Cycle*, the extant volumes number four (as for Wagner's *The Ring*). These four extant volumes also share with *The Ring* the character of a work in prolonged gestation. *Nature*, published in 1977, was republished in 1980 when Morin hit on the expression 'chaosmos'. Here Morin set out the way his organisationalism responded to a universe of order and disorder; *Vie* (1980) developed this organisationalism into a concept of the subject arising from life itself which develops in *Connaissance* (1986) into the concept of a brain-mind capable of matching the contradictions of chaosmos. The spiral is 'completed' in *Idées* where it is absorbed into the 'chaotic' and autonomous world of ideas. My four chapters do not match *La Méthode* chapter for volume since I will extend Morin's spiral by bringing together his 'digressions' on human societies into my chapter 8, 'The Well-disordered Society'.

Chaosmos focuses on a preeminence Morin accords to disorder: implicate order attracts Morin but the philosophic and physical indeterminism of Popper and Prigogine excites him. 'The Subject Reborn' will argue that this bias is only corrected by the organisationalism of the second part of *Nature* in conjunction with *Vie*. 'Chaosmos in Mind' then shows how the brain-mind 'finally' articulates the contradictions of chaosmos in a world of ideas capable of co-existing with chaosmos. 'The Well-disordered Society' draws on the extant chapters on societies together with Morin's earlier sociological writings, to argue that the spiral accords a fundamental primacy to the anarchic aspect of organisation.

The sections in this chapter demonstrate how chaosmos is based on Morin's reading of a crisis in the intelligibility of science and how the human mind can conceive of such a dissolution. The first section characterises the method used by Morin in terms of its three principal strands: dialogic, recursiveness and the concept of the hologram as his path through the crisis. The subsequent sections indicate how Morin came to perceive such a crisis and why the solution he proposes is premised on breaking with Hegelian Marxism intellectually and culturally while also making himself the most Hegelian of all thinkers in the arena of systems theory.

The second section, 'From Chance to Disorder', shows how the concepts of order and disorder first arose from Morin's response to molecular biology and cybernetics.

The third section, 'Order and Disorder', shows that Morin saw order and disorder as pre-scientific, anthropomorphic concepts and yet inseparable in modern science – science and myth connected without loss to either but only because we could recognise that all ordered, determined systems were archipelagos set within oceans of disorder.

In the fourth section, 'The Invasion of Disorders', we see that such unification of science and myth led Morin to a Freudian critique both of Marxism and of 'young Edgar Morin'.

The fifth section, 'Morin's A-Gnosticism', shows that the cultural and historic path Morin took to chaosmos meant he could only accept an implicate order if it was gutted of any connotation of the primacy of order. Thus chaos implies anarchy more than harmony in human affairs. And so the concluding section, 'War over Determinism', analyses the ideological consequences of Morin's ambiguity. He was both an inspirer for those who wished to rescue the fraternalist mythologies of the French Left and a crusader against its institutionalised bastions in 'The University' and the determinism they defended.

## *The Spiral as the Good Circle*

In quoting Heisenberg, 'Method can no longer be separated from its object',[6] Morin prefaces *La Méthode* with a double-layered manifesto.

On the surface it appears to commit him to strategies where the paradoxes of quantum physics are resolved by the agency of the observer. However Morin ultimately seeks not a mind which resolves paradoxes but to open a way of thinking in which thinker and the object of thought are interdependent. The process has to be fully material and fully mental with neither mind nor matter pre-eminent. They are connected as a circuit or loop of which the most basic version is the diagram:

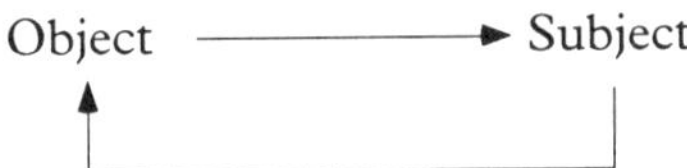


Diagrams of this sort proliferate both in number and complexity in Morin's work. They represent the principle of recursiveness or of process without linear causality to which I shall return later in this section. This diagram indicates that Morin's *La Méthode* will be encyclopedic in a special sense: not as an exhaustive summation of knowledge but an indication that knowledge must circle from the 'objects' investigated by science to the science of knowledge. Morin thus believes that classical epistemology can be included in an extended science of cognition.[8] Hence this circuit is encyclopedic also in including the capacity of physics, biology and the human sciences to serve as starting points from which thought can organise scientific knowledge.

Supposing this were represented as

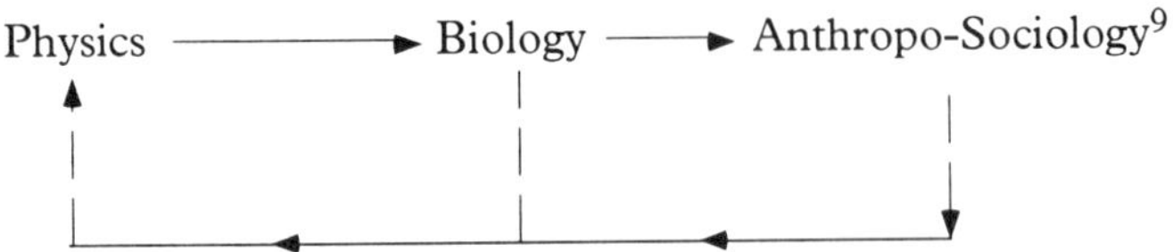

we would see that physics is not a basis for knowledge but, being caught within the recursive loop, actually engenders the problem that knowledge has no basis.

Modern physics, Morin believes, has demonstrated that observation is inseparable from the observer and so rediscovers Bishop Berkeley's dictum, 'There are no unthought bodies.'[10]

Apparently then, all our knowledge might collapse (or be deconstructed) as an overloaded and vicious circle. Logically no springboard exists within the process. Moreover, to have security of knowledge we apparently need both analytically to isolate the sciences and yet retain a synthesising circuit between them.[11] When we add the 'minor' difficulty of the exponential explosion of knowledge it might appear that the only sensible response is a counsel of despair. This was the message given by the academic system, namely 'specialise and abandon all hope of wider thought', to those who enter.[12] Morin by way of contrast will attempt the impossible; his resource is the 'paradigm of complexity' (or complex thought), a method which is not methodology, but a traveller's guide. Its rules are not prescriptive but an aid or way of thinking about complexity.[13] Morin names three principal stands to characterise complexity as a paradigm:

(i) the dialogic;
(ii) recursiveness;
(iii) the hologram.[14]

I shall track complex thought as led by, but not to be reduced to, the dialogic; my procedure claims it as an inverted Hegelianism: Hegelian because rooted in the dialectic, inverted because synthesis is not merely absent but unlikely.

Dialogic is one of Morin's most culturally significant neologisms since it concentrates in itself the distance between English logic and French *logique* ('logic'). Now 'logic' straddles the three senses of *logique* in its real French usage, which as we saw in the introduction are:

(i) the functions of computation;
(ii) the rationalist belief that all elements of an issue are deducible from the concept or idea of that issue; and
(iii) the Hegelian belief that there is a developmental force in a concept such that its implications emerge as successive historical events.

Morin adopted dialogic as a way of expressing the richness of 'logic' in working on the *La Méthode* where dialogic appears throughout contrasted to the dialectic. Thus it did not appear in *Paradigm Lost* of 1973. However, we could cite the inter-dependent relationship of human nature and human culture from *Paradigm*

*Lost* as a usefully simple example of the dialogic;[15] that is, the 'logic' of the dialogic had come to Morin before he adopted the neologism. Morin's dialogic is:

> the complete (complementary/concurrent/antagonistic) association of logics which are collectively needed for the existence, functioning and development of an organised phenomenon.[16]

Because the dialogic does not resolve the conflict of 'logics' it is the most open-ended way in which the dialectic can function.

Morin's reference to phenomena constituted by 'logics' employs this extended usage but expresses its dangers by distinguishing calculation/computation from rationality and rationalisation.[17] Rationality means that logical coherence is attributed to a set of facts or 'empirical reality'. Rationalisation occurs when a totalising, coherent vision of the universe is based on a restricted ground: to explain all human relationships in terms of economic relationships, for example. Now rationality and still more rationalisation are 'closed reason'. To enclose the facts of a field in terms of a single principle such as nature or culture for the human species is insanity. Such a combination excludes anything which cannot be formulated by its principles either as a-rational or irrational. All that reason cannot limit to calculation is rejected; in Morin's list of the irrational we find chance, individuality, and all gratuitous human responses whether 'the feast', art, tragedy or love. To such closed reason Morin opposes open reason that is a complex logic which can be in dialogue both with the irrational and the simply a-rational fact of existence.

The distinction between open and closed reason is heavily indebted to the Frankfurt school of Hegelian Marxists. Morin quotes liberally from Marcuse, Horkheimer and Adorno in his critique of Western rationalism and its desire to reduce all dimensions of existence to computation. And like the Frankfurt Marxists Morin starts from rationalism precisely where it clashes most sharply with empiricism.

For empiricism logical coherence does not require that all the facts of a given issue be deducible from a single principle. Coherence obtains if the facts do not contradict each other. But for rationalism coherence is the same as inference so that all the facts of an issue should be deducible from a principle. Morin as a rationalist rebelling against rationalism concluded that the dialectic is itself contaminated by closed reason. Dialectical thought acknowledged irrationality only so as to capture it for 'Reason'. Adorno glimpsed this paradox when he proclaimed totality to be the enemy of truth.

The concept of dialogic accommodates the dialogue with irrationality and a-rationality to an extent which even Adorno's flexible version of dialectic cannot. Such open reason where different logics can commingle is thus a form of rationalism which can co-exist with empiricism, especially Popper's as interpreted by Morin. So Morin's 'discovery' of empiricism starts from rationalism since he retains the belief that logical compatibility between facts requires the deductibility of all such facts from a single principle. The dialogic accommodates 'Anglo-Saxon' empiricism by emphasising the openness and paradoxical limits of reason. But Morin legitimates this inverted or opened-up rationalism by appealing to its consonance with the crisis of modern science.

Open reason can navigate the environment where science makes reason itself 'bio-degradable'.[18] It is incomplete and constantly challenging itself: 'a method which is not one'.[19] Morin is not only willing to dialogue with mysticism but senses the extent to which empiricism can be open towards acceptance of the mystical. Hence his flirtation with the epistemological anarchism of Feyerabend. 'A method which is not one' alludes to Feyerabend's claim in *Against Method* that objective knowledge is a hoax.[20]

Nevertheless, *La Méthode* undertakes not a dissolution of knowledge but a 'New Science' or a 'science of science'. The dialogic, Morin believes, can transform the vicious circles generated in modern science into good open spirals nourished by these same crises, for if the crisis is 'Hubblean' so is the dialogic. Just as Hubble proved that the expansion of matter in the universe is, paradoxically, accommodated by the expansion of space and time, so Morin's spiral addresses a cosmos where the answers, increasing in complexity, are chasing questions which themselves generate increasing complexity. In the paradigm of complexity the truths themselves change, becoming increasingly complex. In Popper's fallibilism knowledge is definitely 'getting there' although it never 'gets there'; for Morin the method exists but it is a journey on a path where there is nowhere to get to. This appears close to the epistemological anarchism of Feyerabend but for Feyerabend there can be no method since all scientific knowledge, as with Serres, is merely a myth-inspired convention. In contrast even if Morin's goal itself keeps moving, Method, for him, does at least represent the right path.

When combined with the dialogic the other two principles of complexity undermine the likelihood of synthesis. Recursiveness refers to a process where each element can be considered as cause or effect such that a final state might also be an initial state.[21] The physical example Morin invokes comes from Prigogine's analysis of whirlpools which sustain themselves in their instability. Recursiveness also appeals to the indeterminism by which Prigogine explains that some phenomena 'forget' their antecedents so that the concept of cause and effect does not necessarily express progression in time. Now elevated from a property of physical systems to a fundamental principle recursiveness becomes *meta*-physical. It does not only preclude linear causality such as the base superstructure of Marxism. Combined with the multiplicity of 'logics' in the dialogic, recursiveness favours indeterminism and allows a large scope for the improbable.

The hologram concept complements recursiveness towards meeting the problem of knowledge without secure foundation since it combines whole and parts in a relationship which interdicts the reduction of a whole to its parts or absorption of parts by a whole. Just as in a physical hologram all the information about the hologram is contained in every part so the information relevant to every organised totality is encoded in every element although each remains autonomous as well as unique. Recursiveness therefore applies not only to causality between the elements of a system but to information and communication between them and the entire system. On a cosmological level the hologram principle yields the implicate order proposed by Bohm, since the unification of the cosmos, no longer explicable in terms of linear causality, is modelled on that of a hologram, uniting the universe across time and space.[22]

In isolation the hologram principle would therefore draw Morin's 'complex thought' very near to a holism such as Bohm's. Precisely for this reason, however, I argue that the paradigm of complexity is dominated by the dialogic as a result of which no holistic identity of whole to parts will be stable.[23]

In the next chapter we will see that the hologram in the context of organisationalism will function as a paradox. The whole is greater than the sum of its parts and the parts are greater than the whole.

Morin's looping diagrams, of which I have given two simple examples, need to be 'read' through the primacy of the dialogic in the paradigm of complexity. While they illustrate a recursive and hologrammatic relationship between their constituents the presence of different 'logics' ensures that the loop never expresses the identity of its constituents but always, in Hegel's sense, a non-identity of identical concepts.

When we consider the Hubblean spiral of mind in chaosmos in chapter 7, 'Chaosmos in Mind', we shall see how strongly the spiral resists any Hegelian synthesis.[24] Here I indicate that the new alliance Morin proposes between science and philosophy is based on quite different terms of engagement from those he envisaged when he first enunciated the project in *L'Homme*. Science for 'Young Morin' was maid-servant to philosophy charged with the Hegelian Marxist programme of the satisfaction of need. In *La Méthode* science is teacher and mother to philosophy. The scientific advance which exposed the crisis of knowledge without foundation also provided the instruments to navigate in these dangerous waters.[25] We have already seen that this reversal gives Morin bridges both towards Popper's and Prigogine's indeterminist empiricism and to the mystical intuitions of the Tao (of physics). But the indeterminism we find within disorder will give 'implicate order' a peculiar remoteness for Morin.[26] Somewhere beyond the medium-wave there may be harmony but disorder will always predominate in experience.

## *From Chance to Disorder*

The primacy of order and disorder was a terminological legacy of Morin's watershed experience of 1969–70. In 1970 Monod's *Chance and Necessity* and Jacob's *The Logic of the Living* convinced Morin that living cells and hence all the fundamental processes of biology were governed by chemical laws. But, he concluded, molecular biology had actually set up an 'epistemological contradiction', ignored by genetic determinists. They had not, as they believed, explained how chance could be utilised by invariant processes.[27] Morin turned to the work of Prigogine but also to the attempts of cybernetic theorists to explain how living beings used chance differently from artificial machines.

From the conviction that the relationship of chance and invariance could not be explained by the concept of law but rather of organisation Morin perceived chance as an aspect of the wider concept of disorder, and laws of nature as expressions of the wider concept of order.

The laws of nature uncovered by twentieth-century science actually raised a more fundamental question. What was the nature of these laws?

The problem arose from the very successes and language of molecular biology. It was possible to describe the cell as a self-regulating system: it used chemical processes to maintain and repair itself. Monod had used the expression teleonomic to indicate that the cell could only be understood in terms of purpose, even if no conscious agent was responsible for the purpose (in that case we would simply regress to traditional teleology).

The cell could be described as a machine functioning through information and command: hence the expression 'genetic code'. But these commands could only be altered by random mutations since the experience of the cell or living being could not be encoded into its DNA. Thus, evolution could no longer be explained teleologically, that is, by a purpose inherent to the existence of life: mutation was always random. But, Morin argued, Monod had made chance his god, since the very strictness of invariant reproduction left favourable evolutionary mutations incredibly improbable: hence the 'epistemological contradiction'. (In the language of Richard Dawkins, Morin believed that evolution had vastly overspent the statistical probability lent to it by the bank of chance.) Monod had set out to search for India but instead discovered America. Molecular biology had not resolved the mystery of life but did transform the site of its mystery. The question of seeking the life-force disappeared, to be replaced by the problem of how life could make such improbably good use of chance.[28]

The initial attraction of Prigogine's work for Morin was to provide a model of an organised system spontaneously emerging from random events and then sustaining and developing its organisation; from cybernetic theorists Morin encountered the idea that the distinguishing feature of the living cell which artificial intelligence could not reproduce was the ability to turn random disturbance to its advantage. The theorist Von Foerster had termed this principle 'order from noise'. These hints triggered Morin's conceptual revolution which involved expanding invariance into the concept of order, and chance into that of disorder.[29] If this chapter sets out the dialogic of order and disorder the next will show why Morin claims to have unfolded the complexity which allows subjective beings to exploit randomness beyond any probability.

## *Order and Disorder*

Order and disorder are both large concepts; each involves an extended family of meanings. Each family has its roots in an anthropomorphic perception of the world, that is, they are born out of magical-religious concerns to control things, order being control, disorder loss of control. Such an origin is not a shell to be discarded but a core to be enriched. Morin, we remember, takes pride in conceptual contraband and in ridiculing the frontier police of ideas.

The historic origin of order is the human perception of stability in society. At a second stage order is extended to regularities in nature whence it can be formalised at a still more abstract level in mathematically expressed causal relationships. Such order is 'identical with rationality conceived as harmony between the order of mind and the order of the world'.[30]

The anthropomorphic origin of order has therefore been expanded not abandoned. Mathematical formulas are a rediscovery of what magic sought in the spirit.

Disorder is anthropomorphically the shadow of order: randomness is feared and yet ultimately order will need to dialogue with disorder as demonstrated by the problem of chance in biology. Moreover Morin's personal response to this fearfulness of disorder often spills over into an ecstatic frenzy which we can use as a thread connecting his cosmic agnosticism, his flirtation with epistemological anarchism and the anarchic fraternalism of his messianic message.

This section focuses on Morin's classification of disorder. The riches of its texture make disorder plural: order is one, disorder is many.[31] The multiplicity of disorders derives from the recalcitrance of reality to the mind's desire for stability. Hence Morin's classification of disorders already exposes the history of their arrival in human consciousness: the classification and the history broadly coincide in the story of the downfall of 'King Order'. Since the story begins in the mid-nineteenth century, the age of Marx, it expresses a movement which reverses that of Hegelian Marxism. The plurality of disorders – far from moving towards the absolute mind of Hegel or fulfilling it materially – seems to indicate that Western man's consciousness is on the edge of an abyss.

The story begins (in the mid-nineteenth century) when the discovery of the second law of thermodynamics, the principle named entropy by Clausius in 1850, indicated that any closed system suffered irreversible loss of energy. But when Boltzmann in 1877 connected entropy to increasingly random behaviour of molecules entropy came to signify disorder: the degradation of energy was revealed as degradation of order. Far from being able to take order for granted we should now ask: Why is there order rather than complete disorder?[32]

Given that entropy is inescapable, disorder becomes the fundamental problem: if the universe can legitimately be treated as a closed system we need to ask why it has not fallen into complete entropy? The origin and future of order becomes a mystery.

The next level of disorder, introduced by quantum physics, is not only mystery but uncertainty and contradiction since it infects not only the origin but the coherence of order.

Uncertainty came since it was impossible to determine precisely both the movement and position of a particle; contradiction since it was impossible to conceive a particle as both a wave and a corpuscular body.[33]

But there was yet another type of disorder unearthed by quantum physics namely the threat of a vicious circle between the observer and observed, since the act of observation determined whether the particle would be observed as wave or body. The question thus arose whether: 'metaphysical reality escapes our concept of order because it escapes the order of concepts or whether our mind cannot conceive this other order?'[34]

At this level the question posed was not merely how order could exist at all but what sort of order was it which could tolerate uncertainty, contradiction and circularity? But while order had become inherently problematic the challenge so far was localised to particle physics.

In the 'medium-wave' of ordinary physics quantum paradoxes can be ignored. Mathematical formulas thus conceal the breakdown of order.

But at the next level disorder spilt out of the special situations to which entropy and quantum mechanics had been confined. Disorders finish by englobing the universe because both its origin and the knowledge of it suffer epistemological contradictions.

The cosmologies of genesis involve more than competing theories; they force the question of how the mind constitutes theories.

Thus the 'Big Bang' is a catastrophe which carries contradiction in its tail. In catastrophe theory the expression catastrophe signifies an event whose result is unpredictable and hence an 'irreducible singularity'. If the universe has a catastrophic genesis then 'The universal laws are universal precisely in the singular case; they are valid only for our universe.'[35]

The contradictions of such a catastrophe overthrow the limits of our logic. 'The pursuit of rationality leads to absolute irrationality ... time born from not-time, space from not-space and energy out of nothing.'[36]

The universe itself is logically incomprehensible in a way that matches the demonstration by Godel that when strong logical systems are completed they contradict themselves. At its ultimate levels the disorders of the universe and of thought itself are complementary.[37]

## *The Invasion of Disorders*

Morin delights in painting the breakdown of order as a Freudian regression on the part of Western man's historic drive for rationality and control. In this context the chronological coincidence between the age of Marx and the concept of entropy with which order began its breakdown takes on the character of an inversion. For Marx and Hegel time meant development; instead time itself seems destined to be swallowed up in a black hole.[38]

That Morin's attack on the 'adult' consciousness of the West proceeds by inverting Hegelian Marxism not only distinguishes his critique from comparable attacks of Lefebvre, Marcuse or Adorno but makes it a renunciation of 'Young Edgar Morin' including the editor of *Arguments*. Most of the evidence had been available to Morin the Hegelian Marxist. Thus in identifying the Western project of closed reason as an adult persona repressing the insecurity of disorder Morin castigates his own 'adult' Marxism.

The adult solution to the invasion of disorders was simultaneously to ignore and control them. So entropy was dumped into the toilet of the house of Western man where it would not disturb his confidence in evolution acquired from Darwin and Hegel.[39] Order in its primordial sense of control had been assured because the nineteenth century discovered that technology could exploit the concept of entropy to increase the effectiveness of machine civilisation.[40] Since the concept of the universe as a closed system was open to challenge the question 'why is there order?' was dropped as metaphysical ordure.

Even the paradoxes of quantum mechanics could be hidden in the basement.[41] But disorder only erupted well into the twentieth century with Hubble's Big Bang, first heard in 1930 but not confirmed as an explosion until 1965.[42] Thus the moment when King Order was dethroned in Western consciousness coincided with Morin's abandonment of Hegelian Marxism. Morin's story makes him the messenger of the dethronement of order, successor to Nietzsche's madman announcing the death of God. But Morin did not proclaim the death of order. Thanks to the dialogic, order was only dethroned so far as to share the co-production of our universe with disorder:[43] such co-operation requires an englobing or 'macro-concept' – named chaos by Morin.

## *Morin's A-gnosticism*

Morin 'created' chaosmos to express the double function he imposes on chaos as being both origin and the continuing co-production of order and disorder. Chaos in such a sense bears a surface resemblance to the concept of implicate order, illusory precisely because Morin refuses to give allegiance to any one of several theories in physics which allege the existence of other dimensions including consciousness to explain the observed or phenomenal universe. I name his position 'a-gnosis' because he knows there is such a transcendental order but not what it is.[44] The term is my own portmanteau to indicate that chaosmos is 'gnostic' in its commitment to an englobing reality and agnostic in refusing to be committed to any specific theory concerning that reality.

Morin vindicates this ambiguity by contrasting the achievements of modern science with the most agnostic of all philosophies, that of Kant. Kant had drawn an iron wall between the reality we observe (phenomena) and ultimate reality (noumena) of which humans can know nothing. Science has proved Kant right and wrong. It detects a reality beyond the phenomena (Kant was right) but explores and communicates with it through phenomena (Kant was wrong). But where wrong Kant is not entirely so (hence Morin is a-gnostic). Ultimate reality is recognised by thought but exceeds its capacities.[45] Hence Morin refuses to unify the phenomena with dimensions which can be inferred from the phenomena. The only point on which Morin's open reason stands firm is that chaosmos cannot be given the 'logocratic' name of God, even though the Bible writers had grasped that chaos was a problem which overwhelmed logic.[46] Mystery is thus irreducible. But as I indicated Morin's chaos carries an instinctive bias. Morin is happy only with disorder. Not only is the rhetoric with which he depicts chaos appropriate only to disorder but its human implications are overwhelmingly on the side of disorder. The very multiplicity of what physicists term 'grand unification theories' is for Morin a vindication of the need for open reason: their only conquest in that territory is to have rediscovered physics as *physis* in its Greek sense, namely a science which perceives the universe not as an abstract set of laws but of unique things.[47] Morin's chaosmos is a uni-pluriverse – 'uni' because it is unique, pluri because it is open to further complexification – but his emotions are 'pluri' more than 'uni'. There is discrepancy between chiding Michel Serres for exclaiming that only disorder is real[48] and exultation that chaos carries boiling flaming turbulence in her flanks;[49] or that the pluriverse, being disorderly, is a *diaspora* so making the post-genesis universe almost a personal tragedy.

In human terms the discrepancy threatens to congeal into a merger of chaos with disorder since any suggestion of an implicate order behind the turbulence of historical events draws Morin's scorn.[50] If society wishes to repress disorder as 'crime, anarchy and chaos', Morin will vindicate it as fraternity, anarchy and chaosmos.

## *War over Determinism*

Determinism can be upheld or doubted by an empiricist (hence Popper's attractiveness for Morin). But for a rationalist it is a consequence of the belief that facts follow from a guiding principle. The reaction to *Nature* ironically confirmed Morin's insistence that this commitment was a worship of order with all its panoply of religious faith. The religious intensity of the response to *Nature* made it the centrepiece of a battle of the intellectuals such as have punctuated and defined the self-dramatisation of the French intellectuals.[51] Morin's self-perception as messenger of the dethronement of order and his claim to be a saviour from the collapse of determinism provoked reactions which testify to the strength of the rationalism he proclaimed was collapsing. René Thom, the mathematician whose theories of catastrophe as singularities had informed Morin's claim that physics had been regenerated as *physis,* now denounced Prigogine, Atlan, Serres and Morin as purveyors of unscientific irrationality to a public avid for anarchy and disorder. Thom's insistence that science was impossible without a prior, unconditional commitment to determinist laws governing all nature was a juicy example of the rationalist metaphysic Morin had identified as a common ground between Cartesians and Marxists in France. Thom's prestige helped ensure that Morin would remain an outsider in the official culture of 'the University' in France despite the growth of his influence.[52] The house of Descartes stands in France even if its Marxist extensions did collapse, as Morin had predicted. Thus the attacks on Morin allow us to confirm that he is on the cutting edge of the conflict over the rationalism of the French intellectuals but that, not unexpectedly, the death certificate he wrote for it was an exaggeration.

CHAPTER 6

# The Subject Reborn

Claims urging 'the restoration of the subject' were a widespread accompaniment to the crash of structuralism in France. Morin's regeneration of the subject was distinctive not only in his concern for its pre-cognitive, biologically-given origin but the degree to which his organisationalism insists on the creative power of disorder. In terms of the randomness-invariance relationship (see chapter 5) Morin's subjectivism emphasises that the subject exploits the genetic programme it receives. The implication for evolution is to see adaptation as creative rather than responsive behaviour. This version of teleonomy is on the edge of teleology.

The concept which expresses selfhood as a decision-making being in command of its programme is termed *computo* by Morin. This chapter is organised around *computo* which is the key to the unique capacity of living cells. The first section shows why it is, for Morin, the biological ground as well as solution of the Cartesian *cogito*. The second shows why *cogito* requires Morin's organisationalism and the final section will address the problem of communication engendered by *computo* (once again we see that teleonomy is, for Morin, next to teleology).

More broadly, *computo* is pivotal in Morin's rethinking of organisation theory as *re*-organisational.[1] Such a reworking is itself crucial for Morin since self-organisation resolves the order–disorder dialogue in favour of order, although the victory is only provisional. Nevertheless Morin wants to celebrate the victory. When we encounter a new alliance between biology and cybernetics, cybernetics will serve to characterise the creativity of life, not mutilate it to the model of artificial machinery; when we progress from and through *computo* to the relationships between living beings as strategists seeking to survive, Morin will expand the master–slave dialectic into the self-organising relationships of all living beings.

So, the Freudo-Marxism of young Morin will have been transformed in a physicalised Marxism and a biological Freudianism.

The physicalised Marxism is made possible by the use of cybernetics to grasp organisation as self-organisation.[2] In a 're-volutionary' return to the Marxism of his youth Morin extends the concepts of production and praxis as aspects of the re-organising character of *physis*. The prefix 're' becomes a banner for Morin; praxis, which

Hegelian Marxism had made the preserve of human agency, arises in the re-organising, regenerating processes of nature.[3] This alliance of Marx and cybernetics will sharply distinguish Morin from Marxist humanist critics of cybernetics such as Lefebvre.

The biological Freudianism extends the animalisation of psychoanalytical categories we encountered in *L'Homme* and roots them in life itself, that is, in *computo*. By remodelling Freudian categories in terms of communication and information (subordinate to communication) Morin creates a two-way opening. Morin believes he has rescued the concept of information from the dominance of cybernetic and genetic determinism and demonstrated autonomy to be an irreducible property of all living beings. In this chapter I shall also introduce Morin's claims to ground all sociology in the primordial reality of the subject. The degree to which the biological subject makes for autonomy in human minds and human societies will then be explored in chapter 7, 'Chaosmos in Mind', chapter 8, and 'The Well-disordered Society'.

Before proceeding to *computo* I suggest we take along two metaphors to illuminate how re-organisation will enable Morin to switch from the pre-eminence of disorder to the organisational capture of disorder by order. One metaphor is political, organisation being a constitutional sovereignty,[4] the other psychoanalytic since the dialogic of order and disorder, like Jacob wrestling with the angel is 'copulation and a struggle unto death'.[5] These metaphors will remind us that order will never free itself from disorder and that Morin claims that his own uniqueness is to have fully articulated the power of antagonism and death within systems theory.

## *Computo*

*Computo* can literally be translated (from Latin) as 'I compute'. But we shall see that 'I decide' is actually more appropriate.

My note on translating Morin pointed to his 'DNA type' characterisation of life as an irreducibly complex relationship: (geno-pheno-ego) Auto-eco-re-organisation (computing, informing, communicating).[6]

But if this application of the paradigm of complexity to life cannot be compressed, as Morin claims, we can express its two principal elements as *Auto* (or *Autos*) and computing (or *computo*), so grouping the DNA chain into two clusters. Almost graphically we can see that *Autos* looks back and *computo* looks forward; they are two complementary faces of the living self. *Autos* designates the unity of individual (*pheno*), species (*geno*) and environment (*eco*) such that the living being is relatively autonomous,[7] whereas *computo* proclaims the living self to be a 'machine' capable of receiving information, acting upon it and communicating its computations to other selves.

The meaning of *computo* as a decision-taker requires the context of *Autos* which gives life autonomy and so prohibits any determinist reductionism of life. This autonomy will be seen to have deep roots since all beings in their re-organisation have qualities comparable to Heidegger's Being There (*Dasein*),[8] rather than to the objects of Cartesian determinism.

If we start with *computo* as the essential 'I' of all life we shall see its capacities engender the biological roots of Freud's concept of the human persona and also why each *computo* can operate as a social being. The biological capacities of *computo* are at the root of all self-reference. As a decision-taker, *computo* is an 'I' (je) which becomes a 'me' or 'myself' (moi) since all the decisions I take refer to myself: Morin terms such symbiosis 'moi-je'. Physically such self-reference stems from the bodily selfhood (*soi*) of each *moi-je*.[9] It not only can interact with other 'I's'[10] but its physical selfhood expands the anonymity of Freud's *id* since, as *Autos,* it contains the anonymity of genetic inheritance (*on*) and the anonymity of the environment (*ça*).[11] Freud's *id* had animal roots; Morin's will stretch right back into the first bacterium.

But as *computo* the anonymous and autonomous persona is also a decision-taker. The decision it takes with respect to itself makes it self-referential just like Freud's concept of personality but with a crucial difference: consciousness has no part to play in the calculations of *computo* since it calculates not consciously but immunologically since each body can distinguish itself from what is not itself. Thus its genetic programme serves the existential capacity of *computo*. It recognises itself (*soi*), acts (*je*), on behalf of itself (*moi*), in terms of its own survival and by contrasting self and 'not-self'.[12]

Such awareness needs no 'self-awareness' but is 'self-knowledge ignorant of itself';[13] so a bacterium which cannot think or say 'I' acts as 'I' when, immunologically, it recognises itself as unique. We can now contrast *computo* with *cogito* (I think) the usual way of referring to Descartes' 'I think therefore I am', since the allusion is deliberate. *Computo* challenges *cogito*. It exposes within it the biological, Freudian roots Descartes never suspected. That he did not reveals the limitations of *cogito* to be those of Western thought itself, an imperialism of order and mind based on Descartes' myth of modern humanism. Morin's weapons are naturally Western since *computo* exploits the discoveries of molecular biology in terms of the immunological self.

In good company (including Derrida) Morin sets aside Descartes' claim that the *cogito* provided a proposition guaranteed against doubt;[14] he reads *cogito* instead as proof that the individual subject necessarily refers to itself.[15] To identify oneself as 'I' makes two acts of self-reference:

(i) It affirms self-possession: the unique occupation of one's self.
(ii) It identifies this self as the object of 'I''s thoughts, hence as a me or myself (*moi*).

These claims are representable as two recursive loops:

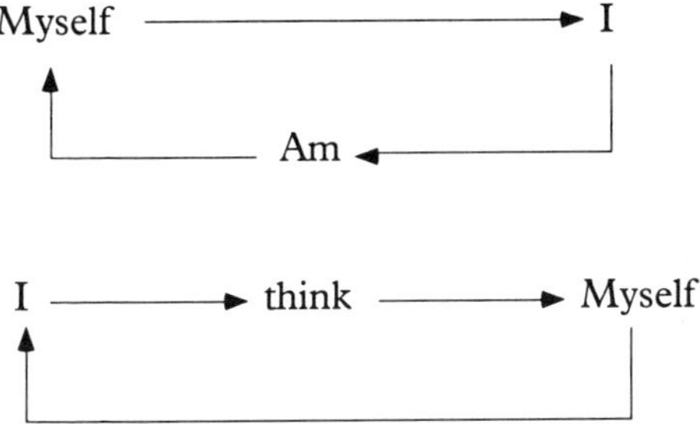


What *computo* solves is the absence of a physical self in Descartes' empty circuits. The self-reference of *cogito* was purely an act of self-consciousness and hence of human thinkers. It threatened an impassable abyss between 'I' and all physics, and indeed between the 'I' and all other 'I''s.[17]

The self-references of *computo*, unlike those of *cogito*, connect 'I' to the bodily self which is the decision-taker. It will remove the 'supernatural' character of mind when it does emerge as a conscious decision-taker since all the elements of self-reference will remain connected in the practice of survival. Moreover immunology endows *computo* with the capacity to recognise 'the other' together with a definition of self. Employing the invariance of the genetic code, *computo* operates with a virtual image of itself which, spectacularly, provides a pre-conscious origin to the double created by human fantasy. Clearly the image does not involve perception but is the immunological capacity of a living individual to recognise its genetic inheritance as a model in the survival strategy. The model is therefore an *alter-ego* or double because it is the ideal body of the living self but not its actual self.[18] In contrast to human fantasies the bacterium is unconscious of its double; nevertheless this unconscious double is at the root of the human capacity both to recognise others and be deceived into the illusion of amortality.[19]

The amortality carried by the genotype (genetic inheritance) is the key which turns the Promethean optimism about amortality of 'Young Morin' into the tragic posture of *La Méthode*, since in *La Méthode* the double will be only a source of fraternity. In *L'Homme* the double arose from the death trauma and encouraged the perception of amortality as an absolute, indefatigable need. But reinterpreted through the genetic code, the double expresses only the amortality of the genotype and is therefore an illusion whose necessity is not that of Promethean conquest but the tragedy of life. Once consciousness translates the virtual reality of its genotype double into the fantasy of the human double, the individual subject is fated for a cruel self-deception, since *alter ego* is indeed amortal but no *ego alter* is amortal. So the individual needs amortality and yet is tragically denied it since it is an illusion. What the double does offer through *computo* is that otherness can be adopted as fraternity.

*Ego alter* is never amortal but is only the other and can be recognised as such by *computo*, beginning with others of its own genotype. So Rimbaud's declaration 'I am another' is as valid for the bacterium as for a human. Identity requires and is enriched by the recognition of others.[20] Tied amortally through the perception of common genotype all living beings are strongly open to the possibility of fraternal community. Certainly all beings are strangers to each other; when in pre-sexual reproduction a bacterium doubles itself the only amortality is that of the genotype: 'The two new beings are two *ego alters* virtually *alter ego* for each other and can become either strangers, siblings or fratricides.'[21]

Nevertheless, fraternity underlies all antagonism because the individual can recognise the other's fraternal identity. Sexuality therefore ceases to be a threat to the need for amortality and can be unconditionally welcomed as the extension of the fraternal unity of the genotype: 'Sexuality adds desire and need to separation. Animals are insufficient beings who, being of one sex periodically then incessantly lack their other half.'[22]

We can easily see that *computo* has transmuted the 'Marxist myth of amortality' into a myth of fraternity comparable to Plato's story of sexuality as the search for a lost other half.[23] To say this would be to hit on the power Morin attributes to the prefix 're', to the extent that one chapter of *Vie* is a hymn to RE. Specifically Morin does want us to accept the genetic code as a myth re-born through modern science. But more generally the anthropomorphism of integrating the genetic code into the fraternal relationships of all biological subjects will reveal the subject to be inconceivable without a concept of re-organisation. Re-organisation allows Morin to plunge back into *physis* from the standpoint of *computo*.

Re-organisation will be seen as the physical key to *computo* since subjectivity is neither consciousness nor a substance but the consequence of organisation. But re-organisation is also the human key to *physis* which cannot be understood outside the humanly imposed concept of organisation.

## *Re-Organisation*

### *The Organisation of Systems*

> 'Because of organisation we can speak of *physis* and yet it is the absentee concept of *physis*.'[24]

Is this, a suspicious English-speaking reader might ask, the game of 'Parisian intellectuals'? Was organisation unknown territory before Edgar Morin explored it?

Morin acknowledges many explorers but believes most have covered only the surface,[25] namely the territory of systems theory and then mistakenly identified the two complementary concepts of system and organisation. But in that complementarity organisation is the core, system the surface. So why has only the surface been visible, the core almost invisible? The surface became the substance of the new science: systems theory was not only associated with cybernetics; the concept of system was the unavoidable consequence of the scientific revolution in which physis replaced the Newtonian eternal laws. So if we accept Morin as a fermenting agent, we have to see both the magnitude of the shift to which the new cosmos commits us and from there advance into the organisationalism working within systems.

### *From the Order of Things to the Nature of Systems*

In the interpenetration of order and disorder the new science had transformed the nature of order. The classical science of King Order was built upon the foundation of discrete things or objects. The new science abolished not just the hegemony of order but the very existence of objects. When the discoveries of quantum mechanics permeated the particle with indeterminacy, the crisis of order became also an identity crisis.[26] In this crisis both object and objectivity will vanish.

First, the object vanishes: the system as generated by quantum mechanics is not built on objects, it dissolves the possibility of objects. Therefore we should not envisage systems as objects, but on the contrary, see objects as systems.[27]

Second, objectivity is dissolved since the system can only be defined by an observer; nature became a complex of systems not merely in the sense that they generated each other but that they referred to and defined each other. Such a 'nature' of systems was thus the contrary of the determinist concept of a unified system of nature. There is not a single system to be grasped by an observer external to it but a plurality of systems. The observer as observing system defined the observed systems but they generated the observer.[28]

We now hold the first key to Morin's concept of organisation. The principle of the hologram operating within a system generates the paradox first stated by Pascal, 'It is impossible to know the whole without knowing the parts and the parts without knowing the whole.'[29]

Pascal is one of Morin's prophets, a rare voice against both holism (the whole cannot be disentangled from its parts) and reductionism (the whole is explicable in terms of its parts). Morin's preliminary definition affirms the irreducible paradox of organisation: 'the agency of relations between elements producing a system with qualities unknown at the level of its elements ... organisation transforms, produces, connects and maintains.'[30]

But now we can see how the recursiveness of Morin's loops will generate a fuzzy identity such that when we read an organisation as a hologram what we will read is not only the identity of whole and parts but their non-identity. Organisation puts Hegel into modern gear: Hegel's concept of identity in non-identity can be represented not only as S (system) =# S but as the double paradox of the system which is both greater and less than its parts:

Their 'resolution' on the level of organisation is the loop:[31]

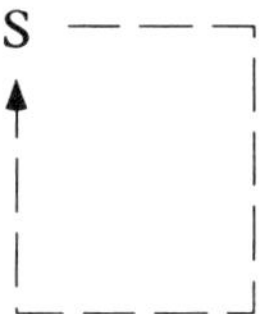


Thus organisation makes a system a continuing process of re-organisation: the system is not itself since it is constantly generating and changing itself. This Hegelian notion has, however, no synthesis; the loop indicates that the change is maintenance as well as transformation. So organisation has the following properties:

1. *Emergence* The elements of a system are not objects: their properties are the relational qualities they hold within the system.[32] They exist only while the system is being maintained or they come into existence when the system is transformed.
2. *Constraint* (servitude). The system constrains its elements from expressing other qualities.[33] The term servitude is both part of the anthropomorphic texture of Morin's language and a reinforced indication that the elements are not objects. It leads to
3. *Antagonism* This property has had its prophets, not only Hegel but more forcefully before him Heraclitus and Marx afterwards. Lupasco, Morin's ally in *Arguments*, had extended

it to *physis* but too schematically.[34] (Chapter 7, 'Chaosmos in Mind', will explain why Morin repudiates any formalisation or logic of contradiction.) Organisationally antagonism is the threat from the elements of a system to de-regulate it: all self-regulatory processes respond to and repress the threat of antagonism prevailing.

4. *Crisis (life and death)* In self-regulating systems crises are developments which increase opportunities as well as dangers, but antagonism will always triumph since entropy ultimately degrades all organisation. Morin's ultra-Hegelian formulation for this tendency is that anti-organisation is 'necessary and fatal to organisation'.[35]

All systems therefore function in crisis and through crisis. In the more complex organisations such as those of living beings the danger of crisis and the ability to use crisis for growth become more developed.[36] So, in the end, all systems perish and the words life and death applied to systems are themselves not metaphors but systemic analogies since they express the difficulty every system has to exist as well as the entropy which will engulf it.

## *The Machines*

In the world populated by the singularities of *physis* the word self (*soi*) also enters as a systemic analogy. An organised system, we have seen, organises itself. A system is not a thing but goes to make up the profusion of selves whom Morin playfully calls 'the extended family of machines'.[37] But this play presents a serious agenda:

(i) An organised system is a machine.
(ii) A machine is a self: in contrast to the object of classical determinism it is a unique entity involved in the production of its own being, so that

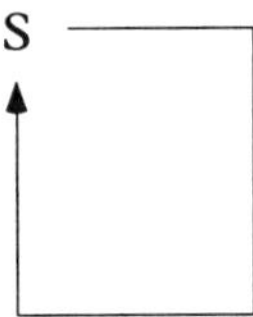


expresses both system and self.

Such an agenda will raise two major issues: why the machine should be rethought as a creative agency and why the creativity of natural machines had been occluded in Western science and philosophy?

The first question returns us to Morin's physicalised Marxism; his response is that of a precursor of the Gaia hypothesis in which the planet is considered as an organised being. Indeed, I suggest, Morin allows us to consider the Gaia hypothesis neither as mysticism nor metaphor but as a consequence of his organisationalist principles in which Marx's 1844 formula 'Man is the producer of Man' is expanded, by Morin, as 'machines are the producers of machines.' (We can see why 'Gaia' is difficult to reconcile with the traditional Marxist refusal to see dialectic other than in human agency.) Under Morin's definition machines not only share in the production but in the creation of their own existence. 'A machine is a physical being practising transformations, production and performance thanks to organisational competence.'[38]

Morin contrasts (favourably) this 'production of self' with the fabrication of objects achieved by the machines of human technology. Indeed the productivity of the natural machine is an aspect of its fundamental performative capacity which is to create. Morin's recourse to the Greek term *poesis* for this creative capacity is connected to an ecstatic hymn to the natural machine, above all the sun, as a 'naked savage'.[39]

So, the second question is solved with the self-production of machines. Western thought could only seek the self as a 'ghost in the machine'. Morin believes he is among the first to see the loop in the machine, where before only repetitive matter had been observed.

The *poesis* of natural machines had been occluded as long as the artificial machine had been taken to be the model for 'the machine'. In fact artificial machines are the poorest examples of the machine. And it is precisely from cybernetics that we learnt of the poverty of technology: the machine of human technology is the only one to be entirely dependent on its producer, human society, for survival and regeneration: in envisaging machines as performative process rather than as the clockwork mechanism of eighteenth-century *Automata* cyberneticians led by von Neumann stumbled onto the fundamental deficiency of all technological machines: they cannot, unlike natural machines, maintain or repair themselves.

Cybernetics, however, could not perceive the resolution of its own discovery: it had dethroned clockwork as the model which all machines imitate, but not seen that the problem lay with the concept of the machine as artefact. Consequently it could not fully utilise its key concept, that of the loop or feedback by which a system is regulated.[40]

In human technology a self-regulating loop has to be programmed; it depends on information which ultimately derives from the social 'mega-machine'. Hence the need for specialised devices to ensure that information is programmed to correct deviation. Natural machines, on the contrary, operate without benefit of specialised devices; the natural machine regulates itself spontaneously so that it is, spontaneously, a 'production of itself'.

The sun, Morin's favourite example, arises from the antagonistic forces of gravitational implosion and thermonuclear explosion such that they do not require regulation; they *are* the self-regulation of the sun.[41]

Freed from its cyberneticist origin the concept of self-regulation is not only recursive but is prior to information not derivative from it, and existential since it is the machine as a whole which creates its being. As an existential being the machine challenges Heidegger's concept of 'Being There' (*Dasein*). Morin takes from Heidegger a refusal to accord 'being' to objects. Heidegger, as the deconstructionist movement enthusiastically emphasised, dismissed not only objects but the consciousness concerned with the production of objects to non-being (a game fit for philosophers and princes). Morin's association with Axelos had left him with this Heideggerean hostility to technology, but his 'Copernican revolution' against Cartesianism 'rescues' the everyday world (*if* rescue is needed): chaosmos, populated by the family machine, is a world of beings not objects.

## *Apparatus*

That life emerges organisationally from the existential, natural machine was hidden by the ruling misalliance between cybernetics and molecular biology. In their joint determinism the metaphoric concept of genetic code was envisaged as a programme emitted by the genes and executed by the living being. Such determinism wrongly thought it had eliminated metaphors; instead genetics used the metaphors of cybernetics so as to engender a double mutilation: both the machine and living machines were reduced to the model of the artificial machine, whereupon this pangeneticism, the Genes Empire[42] was exported to all human sciences in the deterministic concept of the code.

Morin reiterates that the determinist mechanisms must be subordinated to the *poesis* shared by natural machines and living beings. The misalliance, we note, was due not to the use but the misuse of the metaphors of code and programme. In the 'disjunctive' determinism of the ruling paradigm the concepts were badly joined. Morin sees himself as a good joiner. Life inherits from machines not only their existential but their thermodynamic status. Existentially, as in Heraclitus's vision, machines exist by what destroys them;[43] in thermodynamic terms the natural machine is already negentropic, that is, it only exists by reversing entropy:

whereas the genetic-cybernetic misalliance only saw negentropy in informational systems, for Morin it exists in natural or artificial communication.

In Morin's true alliance the concept of programme is subordinated to apparatus, 'the capacity of a communicational organisation to turn information into programme'.[44]

As a 'master concept' apparatus will make intelligible the relationships of liberation and servitude between humans, living beings and machines. Precisely because apparatus pertains both to life and to artificial intelligence it gives Morin the vantage point to develop the opposition of living and artificial apparatuses. The former, *computo*, inherits the existential capacities of natural machines: living apparatus involves the entire self acting on behalf of itself whereas the apparatus of artificial intelligence functions through a special device installed by an external manipulator.

In relationship to *physis*, *computo* is an exceptionally negentropic machine, so exceptional that Morin gradually fades out the expression negentropy but not its sense, namely that life is the most powerful counter to entropy and yet in the end will submit to it. All negentropy is therefore Heraclitean not Hegelian.

Negentropy applies whenever an open system brings in additional energy by borrowing energy from its environment. But this enhancement is paid for by a long-term increase in entropy not only for the system but its environment.

Mainstream cybernetics had wrongly associated negentropy with information whereas it operates in all open systems,[45] since negentropy stems from organisation and information requires negentropy.[46] The reversal of entropy does not, however, permit the Prometheanism of 'young Morin', since negentropy only appears to be the overcoming of an original blockage, that is, negation in Hegel's sense.

Admittedly since entropy is a negative tendency negentropy can be termed 'the negation of negation', but in the dialogic there is no happy synthesis. 'Work in the short run is liberty; in the long run it is death.'[47]

The negation of negation turns out to be not a synthesis but the recursive loop:[48]

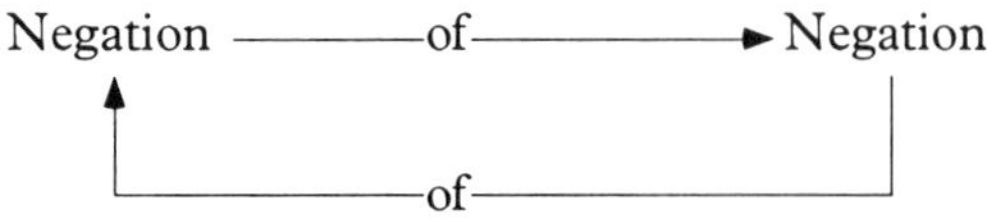


What is lost for Prometheus and Hegel is gained not only for Heraclitus but communication and ultimately fraternity. Apparatus is not only the key to how information serves decision but ultimately to the relationship of freedom and enslavement.[49] To understand and use these possibilities demands that we focus on apparatus as a central problem; it leads Morin to replace Hegel's master–slave dialectic of human consciousness with the problem of autonomy for all living beings.

In the beginning of life apparatus is the vehicle of liberty and communication. The self of natural machines becomes a *computo* capable of dominating its environment: it acts strategically with survival as its initial objective. Such purposiveness is not attributable to the genetic code; the genetic code is to be understood not as state power over the phenomenal self but as an archive, a library belonging to the phenomenal self. In that sense 'teleonomy' is a property of the 'pheno' as much as the 'geno' component of *Autos*. Moreover *computo*'s capacity to recognise with its entire being extends to its capacity to communicate: the absence of specialised command functions in many living forms suggests alternatives to the computer model where communication is only possible through a command centre.[50] It opens up the possibility of envisaging both complex individuals and complex societies as being polycentric or decentralised.

Here Morin does not only instance the relative autonomy of cells within the living body; he seeks to emphasise the 'democratic' character of the brain itself, composed of clusters of operational centres which can either co-operate, compete with, or in certain cases replace each other.[51]

These anarchic possibilities lead Morin to the question which will be the theme of chapter 8: 'Can one imagine and expect the command of communication, a community of communication whose existential development marks the emergence of human love?'[52]

But apparatuses are not only the key to freedom and communication, they are also conduits of all the forms of power. The model of the computer in opposition to *computo* may be mutilating but is not irrelevant, representing as it does the ultimate of determinist power. It alerts us to the full range of apparatuses from the pre-human to the supra-human state and the sub-human computer: through this range Morin lifts the Hegelian barrier against including humans in the general relationships of power between purposive beings. The most general form of power is what Morin names *asservissement*, a term I shall not translate since it carries an all-inclusive characterisation of power which combines 'control' and exploitation.[53] *Asservissement* extends the immunological concept of self: *computo* can make itself an end for itself and treat all that is not self as a means. Even the activity of plants and animals can be represented as a primitive form of unethical behaviour, in Kant's sense of treating others as means for oneself, and hence exhibits the tragedy of all subjective existence.

Through the concept of *asservissement* Morin organises questions of power in terms of information and communication; in societies social and economic problems will be organised in terms of the power of apparatuses. Just as *computo* flings open the constriction *cogito* imposed on selfhood, so through *asservissement* Morin will challenge the Hegelian Marxist belief that the problem of alienation is restricted to human consciousness: the fundamental problem hidden by the master–slave dialectic is that of subjugation, namely when one *Autos* is forced into performing the will of another. (Subjugation applies to *autos* rather than *computo* since the captive being still decides even though it has lost its autonomy in its computations.) Now while only humans are capable of inflicting subjugation they inflicted it on animals before they started on themselves.

The tragedies of apparatus spread far beyond their Hegelian Marxist confines. ('Young Morin', we recall, accepted that alienation resulted from the master–slave dialectic and prescribed amortality as its resolution.) In subjugating animals humans already brought slavery and alienation into play, slavery being the extreme of physical, alienation the extreme of mental subjugation.

> The subjugated autos remains subjectively an individual (a *computo*) but only as the subjugator's satellite ... obedience can be imposed by slavery but also as a law, programme or natural order.[54]

We shall see in 'The Well-disordered Society' how the problem of alienation germinating in the unethical struggles of apparatuses to 'asservice' their environment – materialised by humans as the subjugation of animals – will become critical with the state, 'the apparatus of apparatuses' invented by humans.

We can 'predict' that Morin will be a messenger and a standard-bearer. The message is to illuminate apparatuses in their near invisibility: 'The absence of apparatus from cybernetic, biological and today from social and political theories makes these blind or servile.'[55]

The ruling paradigm of determinism takes the apparatuses of the artificial machines with their specialised command functions as unquestioned models for apparatus. Such determinisms elevate programme over the living subject and, as we saw, trap themselves into the tyranny of codes. Theirs is a vicious circle, not a virtuous spiral.

The depth of the problem of apparatus and *asservissement* could only, in 1980, widen the gulf Morin perceived between himself and Marxist and socialist humanisms. Incapable of seeing self-organising systems except in human societies, incapable of grasping the ubiquity of *asservissement,* even the best such as Friedmann or Lefebvre were too negative in Morin's eyes.[56] They could recognise the danger of *cyberanthrope* (the miscegenation of man and machine), of the cybernetic apparatus as instrument of *asservissement,* but their humanism inhibited insight into the potential cybernetics offered as an instrument of liberation. 'Cybernetics must be transcended so as to realise its revolutionary discovery of organisation through communication.'[57]

What Morin does with this 'programme' is at issue in 'The Well-disordered Society'.

CHAPTER 7

# Chaosmos in Mind

In chapter 5, 'Chaosmos', I characterised Morin's response to physical theories of implicate order as a-gnostic. His concept of the subject allows us to return to Morin's 'a-gnosis' through the reverse perspective, namely, the constitution of a mind-brain which accommodates the failure of any theory to circumscribe reality. Its focal point is two-faced. We discover that no logical procedure exists to 'normalise' contradiction, so the paradigm of complexity is not a formalisation of reality but a path through an unfathomable reality. We discover that ideas are existential beings so the paradigm of complexity is necessary to preserve a sane–insane mind in a logical –mystical universe.

The absence of ontological ground at the physical beginning of the spiral becomes, in the reverse perspective, a matching complexity between 'chaosmos' and the brain-mind. This reverse perspective is the thread of *Connaissance* and *Idées*; the last section of *Idées* runs through the contradictions of the first section of *Nature* but sees them through mind, not *physis*.

There is a relationship of micro–macrocosm between physics and mind but neither can be collapsed into the other since their complementarity is 'unidual'. The universe is unfathomable and mind unfinished. The uncertain navigation of mind through chaosmos reverses the thesis on Feuerbach which had been 'Young Morin's' cornerstone. Man is fated to ask questions he cannot answer.[1] The brain as software is not just a problem-solver but a problem-setter[2] and 'a-gnosis' turns out to be its best organisational strategy.

The adventure begins in the brain which, in its human stage, is the most complex being in the universe unless it is the universe which produced it.[3] Due to this 'hyper-complexity', *esprit*, which I translate as 'mind', emerges from brain as the capacity both to think and to think of self.[4] (Once again we see Morin exploit the rationalism of the French language. 'Esprit', like German *Geist*, means both mind and 'the spirit' so that, in French, mind cannot be decontaminated from the unseen viewer who scans the brain computer.) Such emergence is doubly mediated. Brain-mind is integrated by human society's possession of culture stored (not coded) in language (see 'The Well-disordered Society') but culture is a possession for individuals who employ it.

It is in these conditions that the brain-mind loop activates the *computo-cogito* loop.

That individuals and societies co-operate in the loop which connects them to brain-mind is indicated in diagram (a), while the biological loop which engenders brain-mind is indicated in diagram (b).

(a)

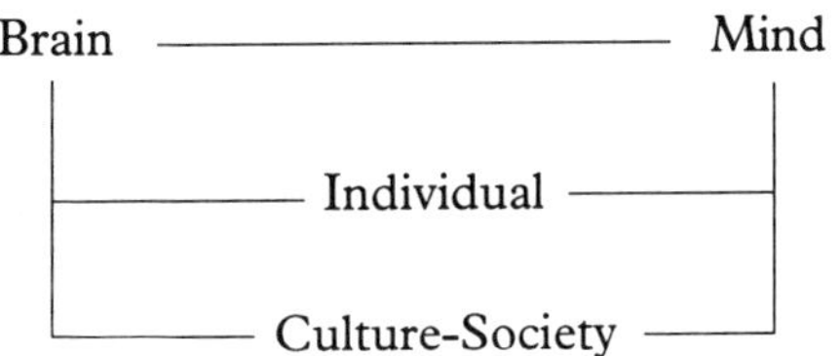


(b)

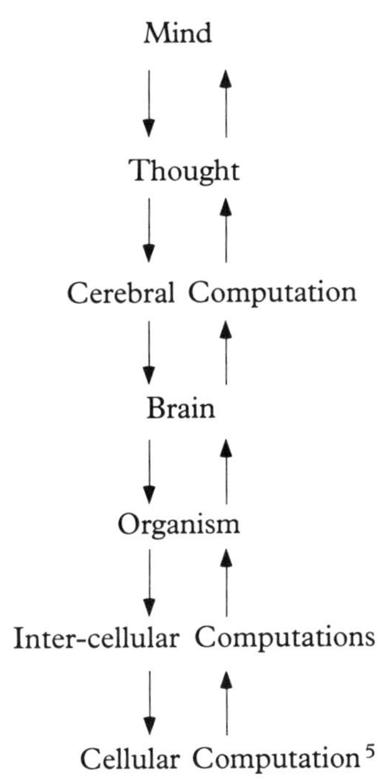


From (b) we observe that *cogito* does not oversee or found the unity of self from a transcendent point above but emerges from a chain of biological computations of self in which the self is organised anarchically, heterarchically and hierarchically. This emergence can be represented by a further diagram (c),[6]

which illustrates how Descartes had unconsciously built *cogito* upon the biologically computed multiple unity of the self. Having grounded thought in self-computation Morin claims brain-mind to be equidistant from materialism and idealism. Both are necessary, both are insufficient. Mental states and brain states are unidual in a contradictory unity of the identical and non-identical. The mind is so autonomous that it produces seeming miracles upon the brain, yet so dependent that ten seconds' loss of oxygen causes irreparable damage.[7]

Even before culture intervened *homo* had the capacities to be *sapiens demens*.[8] But error built into *computo* as an apparatus proliferates with the act of perception into irreducible uncertainties. The brain stimuli which mind constructs into images are identical before mind decodes them as being real or hallucinatory. The two strategies mind employs in decoding, namely the 'empirical-logical-rational' and 'the symbolic-mythological-magical' do not provide mind with any certain criteria of reality: all we can say is that the first strategy corresponds to the existence of a three-dimensional Euclidean world but we also know how uncertain that world is:[9] 'The reality we know is both strange and familiar.'

The two cognitive strategies employed by mind are inextricably tied in a 'uniduality of the real and the imaginary', analogical to the yin-yang of the Tao.[10] Diagram (a) indicates that such uniduality will operate both through individuals and society. We can begin either at the level of individual cognition with the relationship of the logical and the analogical or, on the level of language, with the relationship of *logos* and *mythos*. In both instances it is not possible for one path to exclude the other (the rationalist strategy) nor even to formalise the left-hand path (the strategy of holism and organised mysticism) so as to produce a legible implicate order.

There is, to begin at the level of individual cognition, no logic of analogy, but a dialogic between logic and procedures which can be sub- or meta-logical. Analogy is in fact an umbrella for a number of procedures which share with logic the computational core of binary choice: the mind has to decide either to accept or reject an analogy just as it has to accept or reject a logical inference. The disjunction between them is produced by our culture in which scientific thought scorned analogy even while it employed analogies.[11] The theories of cybernetics have, however, forced the dialogic into the open since certain kinds of analogies, namely those of form and organisation, have been adopted in systems theory as with the use of the concept of feedback for artificial machines, living organisms, eco-systems and societies.[12]

At the socio-cultural level the two cognitive strategies generate two worlds – *logos* and *mythos*. Morin employs the Greek to indicate that *logos* is not only logic but empirical-technical-rational, *mythos* not only myth but symbolic, mythological, magical.[13]

On this level we encounter uniduality apparently embedded not in *computo* but in language. These two worlds (*logos* and *mythos*) are one because words are both signs and symbols so that to separate these functions as signs for rational discourse and symbols in mythological narrative respectively will prove a forlorn enterprise. The essential nature of symbols is to coagulate word, meaning, sense and reference so as to become a proliferating jungle which myth arranges by turning all events into messages.[14] Instrumental thinking seeks to immunise itself against such proliferation but it cannot be decontaminated, as Morin boldly proclaimed in subtitling *Les Idées – Their Habitat, Life, Morals and Organisation*. Through words ideas are existential beings: they have their own ecology comprising the individuals who house them (psychosphere) and the socio-culture in which they are used (socio-sphere). Their life depends on this ecological support but is nonetheless autonomous, a noosphere with its own organisation or no-ology. Initially, Morin had intended to title this volume *Noosphère et Noologie*,[15] thus openly proclaiming a verbal debt to Teilhard de Chardin[16] who created the word noosphere to express an unorthodox, mystical-Catholic evolutionism.

The relative autonomy of ideas is not God-given (it depends on its human ecology) but is nevertheless 'God-like': 'We can understand why Hegel makes humans servants of the idea.'[17]

The fertility of their lives comes through the repressed forces of analogy and myth. Human language, 'the most radically alive element in the noosphere', is organised on principles analogous to those of the DNA code,[18] and the DNA code operates on the principles of the double and metamorphosis which are those of myth.[19] (The double is the biological root of myth and the route between myth and biology.) When, with the Vienna circle's attempts to create an artificial symbol-free language, logical empiricism made its supreme effort to be rid of contamination, it only helped expose the full extent of the breach.[20] (As in all myth stories about the hubris of knowledge from Babel to Oedipus.)

These breaches, already encountered in chaosmos, had generated the method of self-organisation. But *Nature* seemed to leave unanswered the possibility of a mind which could unify contradictions in a higher implicate, order (as many physicists believe).

In *Idées*, returning to contradictions, Morin's answer becomes unequivocally 'no'. He distinguishes three sorts of contradiction.[21] The 'lowest', easily set aside, are simply the product of bad reasoning; a contradiction in this sense closes or ruins an argument. In contrast there are contradictions which open onto a hidden dimension or meta-view. But open contradictions themselves branch out into 'weak' and radical.

The weak can be surmounted in complex thought and thereby incite towards dialogical thought. They ruin the certainty of deductive, syllogistic thinking otherwise termed by Morin in an expression taken directly from Castoriadis but ultimately from Hegel, 'The logic of identities': [A = A, A = not A].

But radical contradiction confronts us with 'the limits of understanding'. Reality itself might not be contradictory; our understanding of it has to be so.[22]

Hence Morin parts company with Castoriadis and other theorists who have attempted to formalise a 'logic of non-identities', precisely because they would place bounds on 'the enormity of the real'. To accept and integrate contradiction does not solve it.[23]

For Morin not only reason but non-reason is 'biodegradable'. The value of any method such as Hegel's dialectic was not as a new logic, but in having founded a philosophic approach capable of recognising ambiguity and contradiction. Hence *La Méthode* is not a higher logic but uses logic in its separate operations while accepting that their totality escapes it. According to the complexity of 'the real' logic is sometimes surmounted, sometimes transgressed, and sometimes weakened.[24]

When the brain-mind explores reality we discover that Morin's paradigm is the reverse of all previous paradigms; they had been epistemes confirming or formalising the movements between thought and reality; only in complexity is logic preserved while the mysteries beyond the medium-wave are both exposed and unsolved.

CHAPTER 8

# The Well-disordered Society

Morin is a sociologist at war with his discipline:[1] bio-socio-anthropology overspills sociological theory since it proposes to incorporate human societies into the range of all societies as they occur amongst all living beings.

The sociology of *La Méthode* is therefore the apex of a reforged teleology where the possibilities of the human species are celebrated. While the Promethean drives for the satisfaction of need have been discarded, Morin's sociology is about the subject both in its individuality, irreducible to social roles, and its inheritance of multiple *asservissements*. Fraternity is the bearer of Morin's restless and complex utopianism. Its combination of emergences and possibilities makes the organisational dimensions of human species hypercomplex. As an emergence it had been generated by the biological subject which however is incomprehensible except through the perspective of human society. It is also an emergence from societies, 'entities of the third kind', all of which exploit the informational capacities of the biological subject. But the human species is also hypercomplex because it has the possibility of becoming an entity of the fourth kind, namely humanity. Messianism is therefore *organisationally* inseparable from Morin's analysis of human societies since these bear potentialities which can lead either to humanity or to the apparent triumph of an 'asservissing' apparatus modelled on that of artificial machines.

These alternative destinies operate on a number of levels.

(a) That of a bio-political choice which the human species must make, not only in terms of its biology but of its relationship to the biosphere. These options can be represented as a debate between the Left and the Right where Left and Right are political on the surface but biological in their full meaning. The Left is the option of greater complexity, the Right is the warning that the safe limit may have been passed. Morin declares himself of the Left but accepts that the Right is as eternal as the Left.[2] Left and Right are ultimately principles of organisation and so are both 'immortal' just as love and death are 'immortal powers' for Freud.

(b) In terms of the history of human societies the tension concerns the opposing 'logics' of the centralised apparatus of the state and the expansive 'logic' of culture as the uniquely human form of a genetic archive. The dominant tendency is for the state apparatus to *asservisse* culture especially in the crucial model of the nation-state:[3] the French version *État-nation* is conceptually more powerful since it indicates that states make nations. This capture is however reversible; hope lies in the range of apparatuses generated by living organisations.

(c) Anarchy versus Hierarchy. The state model of apparatus, taken from artificial machines enfolds three aspects of command: Hierarchy, Specialisation, Centralisation.

Morin's strategy seeks to demonstrate that this hierarchic model not only requires anarchy but that anarchy is prior to and more creative than the centralised, hierarchy model of command. Now there is a force which traverses all these levels and encourages Morin in his optimism: it is that of fraternity, which, we remember, is born in the division of life itself as the relationship between *alter ego* and *ego alter*, the genotype and the stranger. In human societies it turns into a psychoanalytic myth, 'Romulus', favouring the emergence of the 'fourth kind' entity, humanity, so that fraternity is the thread between bio-Leftism and the culture of the French Left.

My exposition begins with 'the biological crisis', and then discovers two stories which meet in it: 'Asservissement', and 'Anarchy', before they resolve in 'The Brotherhood of Man'. Much material is drawn from *Vie,* especially its 'digressions', the chapters on 'Societies', and 'Man Alive', which, I suspect, are the motifs of the undelivered volume on Humanity. (It is not only the method but the texture of *La Méthode* which recalls Wagner's Ring.)

## *The Biological Crisis*

> The fundamental vice of all Utopias is to envisage the elimination of disorder, uncertainty, conflict, antagonism ... this ignores the principle of entropic degradation and of complexity ... The dystopias rightly present violence, conflict and death as *liberation*. The 'good' society based on liberty will be in permanent regeneration, the 'good' revolution in permanent revolution.[4]

Morin's spiral requires that the permanent increase of disorder and antagonism be transformed into invention and freedom. Recognising the doubts that such a message trails Morin divides the possible answers, and himself with them in ... the Left and the Right. The Left is the hypothesis that the hypercomplexity and the disorder inherent in equality can be further extended, so indefinitely weakening 'domination, hierarchy, power and realise the aspirations of liberalism, libertarianism, socialism and communism'.[5]

The Right believes that our crisis of civilisation is a warning for a return to order and that hypercomplexity brings disintegration.

Conservatism wants to rely on the genetic programme (heredity, tradition), not individual strategy. In naming these alternatives 'Left' and 'Right' Morin reaffirms his spiritual membership of the French Left. Indeed one might object that his membership is too spiritual since the list of values 'liberal, libertarian, socialist and communist', represent a communal summa of the great historic battles fought by the French Left but are hardly capable of being reconciled in a single programme. On the contrary, while the *Programme commun* of the socialists and communists was attempting such a conjuring act, at the very moment when *Vie* was being written, Morin's response combined extreme scepticism and sceptical hostility.[6] The economic rationality which could underpin such a combination should be examined in the context of the bio-physical dimensions Morin attributes to the alternatives of Left and Right. For Morin's objective is to demonstrate that the values of the French (and Western) Left will appear dislocated to conventional political science, sociology or economics but will begin to come together in the broader perspective of auto-eco re-organisation.

The fundamental issue and perspective is that of using disorder. The relationship of entropy to negentropy ensures that equality and liberty can be reconciled, because where there is a maximum of disorder, a minimum of constraint, there is also a maximum of equality in an organisation. Hence the conflict of Left and Right is grounded on the opposition of order and disorder to which the oppositions of equality–inequality, liberty–authority are all secondary.

In terms of ideological positioning, Morin's meta-perception of the Left–Right oppositions as that of order–disorder placed him on the Left but not within the Left in 1970s' France. As indicated, Morin believed his interlocutors to be the philosophers of the new Right (former 1968 Leftists who, after their break with Marxism, emphasised the biological roots of human conflicts and hierarchies). On the Left his allies remained primarily Castoriadis and Lefort, at least until the crash of Marxism converted the Left nearer to Morin. Morin sees himself playing on the same field as the new Right: with them he grasps that the fundamental issue is a biological crisis in our civilisation but he bets on a hypercomplexity they bet against.[7]

If hypercomplexity plunges humans into permanent crisis,[8] Morin's common ground with the philosophers of the new Right is to see that a moment of decision has arrived with the genetic control of life, birth, death and intelligence:

> We are at a decisive phase when man takes a power over life which will be as controlling and uncontrolled as power over the atom. Its two principal avenues will be action upon genes and

> upon the brain such that the spirit will retroact upon the emergence of its physico-chemico-biological qualities.[9]

The opportunities and dangers born of the bio-crisis will therefore retroact on all the social instances at which our biology is explicitly socialised. 'The perturbations which affect the notions of father, mother, child, of masculine and feminine, of all that is fundamental to the family and society [now] requires political regulation.'[10]

In specific issues of bio-ethics Morin respects the 'eternal' enemy since bio-ethics will involve killing and experimentation of which Morin is extremely chary.[11] The direction in which he will sway requires that we untangle the knotted relationship between fraternity and fratricide. But the caution here is easily comprehensible when we remember that all bio-ethics for Morin takes place in the shadow of the state apparatus. If its prospects are exalting they are also terrifying once the question of control is posed and answered by its location with anonymous apparatuses of which the culminating, apparatus of apparatuses, is the state.

> The individual will not control his own brain. Once more scientific power, dislocated at the research level, will concentrate itself as a social praxis at the level of state power.[12]

So the crisis as a moment of decision takes Morin back to the decisive instance of apparatus in the control of information. We can hence measure the extent to which Morin's bio-Leftism operates on a terrain where his bridges are to the new Right and his ideological scourges are of the traditional Left, including therein the 'Young Morin' of *L'Homme*. The dangers all stem from the imperialism of successful command, beginning with the command of nature, denounced by Morin as the 'barbarian myth of the conquest of nature'.[13] The command of nature by man rebounds on humans as the command of man by man through the force of the apparatuses which charge themselves with the execution of such 'Ghengis Khan' imperialism. Whereas the problem of apparatuses is ignored by the dominant ideologies of the Left, Morin has two stories to tell, the first that of the *asservissement* of organisation by centralised apparatuses, the second that of the potential unravelling of this *asservissement* by the reorganising power of anarchy culminating in the victory of fraternity. In telling the story of Apparatus triumphant, first I respect Morin's general penchant to tell stories of regeneration against the odds.

## *Asservissement*

The dangers of *asservissement* are implicit in the polemical stance Morin adopts to introduce his 'sociology'. Against the dominant ideologies he insists that human societies must not be dissociated from those of living nature. Nature and culture, as we saw, exemplify the dialogic at work since human societies are fully natural and fully cultural.

> We must break the disjunctive vision where man is biological only through body and genes, and social in mind and society ... My anthropo-sociology will not introduce pan-geneticism, socio-biology or organicism but be open to a complex vision of life.[14]

In the first instance human societies are simply societies. A society is a complex organisation, but not an organism, derived from its members, who are, as animals, entities of the second kind. Society is not an imposition upon the interaction of individual subjects since these interactions constitute it. But society is more than the sum of these interactions since they produce a social system, an organisation which retroactively organises and controls the production of these interactions and assures its homeostasis through the turnover of individuals who arise and die. All societies draw their organisational qualities from those of entities of the second kind: as systems they do not only organise their members but are organised by them.

In chapter 6, 'The Subject Reborn', we encountered Morin's emphasis on the strategic capabilities of the animal: an individual of the second kind is primarily comprehensible not as a programme ordering a strategy but as a strategist employing a programme. A society of such beings cannot be conceived as an organism with a rigorously overriding central apparatus: it is always an organisation. Now an organisation cannot usurp the autonomy of its members but, on the contrary, can only exist where individual subjects are endowed with a significant level of autonomy.

The irreducible autonomy of its members imposes a major organisational and ontological constraint on all societies: they are fundamentally incomplete. Societies do not dispose of an autonomous apparatus; they function with a quasi-apparatus. Such imitations became palpable to nineteenth-century ethologists in the case of insect societies which mimicked the existence of a centralised apparatus and, as with bees, installed a pseudo-*computo* in the shape of the queen bee. But since such pseudo-apparatuses were only possible with a minimal level of member individuality, animal societies, whose members possess greater individuality, were not until recently recognised as the societies they really were by human observers.[15]

### *The Savage Economy*

The closeness of societies to eco-systems invites us to investigate the eco-system as a self-maintaining organisation. Using the Greek term *oikos* Morin exploits the echo between *oikos* (economy) and *eco* (ecology). The bio-system is a 'jungle', an entirely unregulated economy, in which the balance sheet involves not the production of goods but the production of individual subjects.[16] In this anarchy life and death feed each other and feed from each other so that the excessiveness of life is balanced by that of death, and disorganisation from death is met by the reorganisation of life. In a non-mythical sense, Morin says 'the Eco-machine is an Osiris in permanent disintegration and rebirth.'[17] The disclaimer cannot disguise the emergence of a new myth which 'at least' explains the ways of death for Morin: I reserve the analysis of this myth until we have explored fraternity.

### *The Practice of Life*

The eco-machine involves its members in a new form of praxis, far more complex than that of natural machines. The process of maintenance and transformation proceeds on the basis of the strategies of individual subjects so that the biosphere is a practice which involves information and communication as well as *asservissement*. For the individual subject this means that in maintaining and transforming itself it is also maintaining and transforming the environment. Morin's emphasis on the concept of auto-eco re-organisation attempts to indicate that *computo* has to establish strategies which concern both itself and its environment.[18] Such computation is clearly not an environmental consciousness any more than *computo* is self-consciousness; while the beings of the biosphere are not small 'Greens', nonetheless an unregulated praxis operates between them. Between individual subjects the praxis of the eco-system involves complementarity and *asservissement*. This relationship of informational *asservissement* pervades all economies. That control precedes production will prove to be the case for human economies, as for 'the savage' spontaneous economy of the *oikos*. The primacy of control and information exposes the limitations of Marx's pre-cybernetic concept of production. Restricted to the science of his day Marx could only understand production in terms of a physics based on energy. Beyond such a concept of power:

> What matters in not power over the means of production but power over the production of production, namely the generative capacity of society ... mastery resides in the *asservissement* of the means of *asservissement*, the informational power of apparatus.[19]

And hence the humanisation of the human animal is above all the story of control, beginning with the control of the environment. In *Paradigm Lost*, Morin's history of the natural-cultural process of the emergence of the human species, control takes precedence over the tools of control. 'Asservissing' other life forms, as with the domestication of animals, or the increasing store of agricultural knowledge, is central to the store of culture out of which production of objects becomes possible.[20]

*The Avoidable Rape of Culture*

The process of *asservissement* finds its penultimate phase in the creation of nation-states, apparatuses capable of exploiting the already huge capacities human society had generated for the spread and control of information. (The ultimate version of apparatus, the totalitarian state will be analysed subsequently.) The French expression 'state-nation' is ideal for Morin's insistence that apparatuses of control intervene in all the civilised stages of the 'social mega-machine', a term he borrows from Lewis Mumford. Beginning with the creation of cities and states the social mega-machine is a complex of apparatuses which in the human context are institutions monopolising or striving to monopolise information and communication. Its ability to capture the cultural archive of humanisation allows the social mega-machine to put its roots down in the spontaneous relationships of the *oikos* and convert them into instruments of control. It was, however, far from inevitable that the state apparatus should take control of culture. Human societies had worked well by culture alone because culture was not code or programme but a capital or inheritance: there was a complex relationship between culture as a programme and the competences of individuals: we had to see such competences not only as generated by programmes but as generating them; we had to remember that culture was stored in the mind, not in genes, and was thereby always a personal capital.

> Culture is an informational patrimony comprising knowledge, skills, rules and bans concerning environment, techniques, rules of sharing food and women, a world view and rites wherein the community affirms and regenerates itself. Culture is a social capital precisely because it is not a biological inheritance.[21]

It is therefore not enough to see that culture is both an individual inheritance and a social capital. It is not enough to say that culture is a process in which human individuals and human societies were formed and that the cultural *genos* co-operated with the biological in producing the human species, since only the enlarged human brain could accommodate culture and only the cultural humanoid could find the enlarged brain with its delayed maturity an evolutionary advantage.[22] What needs further to be seen is that culture is the decisive evolutionary step in the history of societies, since human societies, exceptional in possessing culture, are nevertheless 'only' a part of all societies which, as entities of the third kind, include all animal communities.[23]

The complexity of generation between culture and the individual, species and social genetic inheritance interdicts all structuralist schemes in which culture and nature are opposed. No event in humanisation represented a point of transition between nature and culture.

The decisive instance invoked by Morin is that of generation itself, of sexual reproduction as a cultural inheritance. Morin's attack bears both on the Lévi-Strauss and the Lacan versions. The structuralists not only fail to see that sexual culture is inscribed in the wider self-production of the human species but fail to appreciate the co-operation of genetic and cultural inheritance in the formation of the personas of human sexuality. For Morin the decisive instance opposes fraternity to the 'the father', the image on which structuralist psychoanalysis was feasting in the 1960s and 1970s. Morin's banner in his close encounter with Lacan is 'the name of the brother', whose messianic implications for fraternity emerge in the ultimate section of this chapter.

In the Lacanian vulgate 'the father' carries *the law* under which the name of incest passed upon son–mother intercourse also makes it the unthinkable foundation of human society. The father as the only person who can transgress the ban on the mother thus monopolises the power of the law (society) even when the biological relationship of paternity is not recognised. *Oedipe* (the Oedipus complex) stands above cultural accident; valid for all human cultures *Oedipe* is a virtual reality which supersedes our biological inheritance since the father becomes the metaphysical concentrate of the creation of society (God), power over society (the ruler), and sexual power in society (patriarch).[24] (Louis Malle's film *Le Souffle au coeur* found the extreme solution of legitimising mother–son intercourse). Morin's bio-anthropology dissolves the monopolistic claim of the father to erect a frontier between nature and culture. In the history of humanisation the 'archival' recognition of fraternity precedes that of mother–child relationship; the father, 'a latecomer to the Holy Family',[25] is converted by Morin from creator to expropriator of social power, who slides into the 'authority of the leader and the sacredness of God'. It is not simply that paternity was a late discovery of human culture (Lacanian psychoanalysis was designed precisely to discount this embarrassing cultural fact) but that it occupied already existent social roles. Fraternity is central to Morin's dissolution of the father figure; it is a social relationship but we should not forget its biological depths in the 'fraternal solidarity and communication between *ego alter* and *alter ego*'.[26] In societies fraternity is engendered not only by communal bonding against external dangers (the environment, other species, other societies of the species) but by struggles for domination within the society. Now neither biological nor social fraternity is literally a sibling or brotherhood relationship. If biological fraternity derives from the pre-sexual capacity to recognise the *ego alter*, social fraternity derives from the capacity the members of an animal society have to recognise each other: community rather than fraternity. Fraternity only becomes brotherhood when human societies invoke it as the mythological source of their unities and disunities. It is therefore both real and mythological: 'individuals believe themselves generated by a common ancestor and hence to be fraternal ... but with the forces of disintegration our societies are based on fraternity and its self-destruction.'[27]

The common ancestor is, however, not a father (Abraham) but the society itself, organised as a community or a city: it can thus be mythically represented both as brotherhood and as a mother–child relationship.

The story of Romulus and Remus demonstrates the mythico-real foundation of the community.[28] (Romulus and Remus are twins but their parents are nameless and their mothering nurse is a she-wolf. They build Rome, quarrel, and Romulus kills Remus.) The myth, Morin claims, combines fraternity and fratricide as the origins of the community. Social roles are both mythical and natural: they precede 'the father' and his law. Human leadership emerges as the mythological dimension of the dominant male in animal societies who is simply *Big Brother* and who presides over the initial distribution of goods (including women) – the father slips onto Big Brother's seat. Morin's characterisation of society as mythico-real is, I suggest, eminently invertible: society is natural just as it is mythic. The point of this inversion becomes clear when we relate Morin's 'mythico-real' to that of Castoriadis in *The Imaginary Institution of Society*.[29] Despite their alliance against 'structuralo-Marxism' and 'psycho-structuralism' they were respectively Morin on the naturalist, Castoriadis on the culturalist flank of their mini army. Morin's myth followed Castoriadis in the emphasis on 'the imaginary' as the founding action of human societies; for both a crucial moment arrives when the community creates itself in its own imaginary image and so comes to occupy the site of a (social) being from which all others are excluded. But for Morin the myth has a real origin – fraternity – and hence will be revealed to have a potential destiny: fraternity.

Between the archival fraternity of culture and the possibility that fraternity could generate a being of the fourth kind lies the reality of the capture of communities by apparatuses of control. This capture transforms communities; their identity becomes that of a nation.

*State Apparatus*

In Morin's language the state is born terrible.

> A multidimensional central apparatus, the sovereign state produces and monopolises information, occupies the socio-centric site of a *computo*, commands formidable temporal and more so spiritual instruments ... under its control the social machine increases constraints through the specialisation of labour so inducing a generalised regression of individual autonomy.[30]

This is a retrospective apocalypse; despite the inherently incomplete character of all sociability, the state is a monster with a fully fledged apparatus; its personality is so palpable for Morin as to allow him to envisage that its apparatus identity and personnel collude in an inner logic which can ride out the perturbances of the social mega-machine. On one level there is complementarity. The 'logic' of the state collaborates with the eco-logic of the social *oikos* to produce dominance and exploitation so that the state works in symbiosis and mutual parasitism with the dominant class. But the monstrous persona of the state carries another 'logic', that of a *computo* which nourishes itself on the disorder and re-organises itself in conditions of extreme instability. 'Individuals, factions and groups struggle to control the state; state authority always infested by particular interests is not always recognised by all as the authority of all society.'[31]

Nevertheless the conflicts, divisions and ecologies of society contribute to the state's development in disorder with, as its (penultimate) success, the rise of the 'state-nation'. If the state is a being the nation-state is doubly alive. The nation is the state's reshaping of the imaginary institution of society. Certainly, it only exists, like the gods, through our actions. Nevertheless, like the gods, it is endowed with the super-reality of myth. Thus, in 1980, Morin could fulminate against the blindness of sociologists who, besotted by questions of interest (*Gesellschaft*), missed the complexity and intensity of the nation as a product and producer of community (*Gemeinschaft*). If Morin's invective is less appropriate to more recent tendencies in sociology Morin can – and has – claimed the post-1980 upsurge of nationalism as vindication of his prophecies.[32] Developing the myth-realism of communities nations are not simply the arbitrary play of the imagination; they are myths steeped in the *genos* of human societies combining the functions of nourishing, beloved mother and authoritative father so as to reactivate the fraternal impulses of defence and sacrifice.[33]

## *Anarchy Below*

The story so far of the state-nation is that of a being 'more real than reality' since it is apparently a complete myth entity, anthropomorphic (created by human language), theomorphic (humans make it divine) and cosmorphic (its territory is an entire world).[34] But the 'logic' of *asservissement* retroacts so as to constitute not one but three 'logics'; the nation-state as a force of *asservissement* and subjugation produces a 'logic' of developing the individuality of its members, and these constituted rights tend to become existential claims. The individual subject not only claims freedom under and against the state but freedom from the constraints of his biological *genos*.

The social *oikos* (the economy) also had its own logic despite its *asservissement* by the nation-state.[35] The balance of competition and complementarity between these developments is decided by the alternative ways in which apparatus can function as represented by the following grid:[36]

> Specialisation–Hierarchy–Centralisation
> Poly-specialisation–Heterarchy–Polycentrism
> Non-Specialisation–Anarchy–Acentrism

The central opposition can be seen to be that of hierarchy–anarchy; the other oppositions do not reduce to the hierarchy–anarchy contrast but are grasped in its terms. And while the state benefits from the apparent self-evident virtues of specialisation, hierarchy and centralisation, even the competence of this model requires an underlying anarchy; the force or 'logic' of such anarchy derives from the self-organising nature of organisation. Anarchy is defined by Morin as: 'organisation in the process of birth and self-sustenance, without superior authority, based on the intercommunication of computing beings.'[37] Retroactively an organism retains anarchy even while it imposes command, hierarchy and centralisation.

Morin's anarchy is not necessarily apolitical but is ontologically prior to politics. It is disorder, which we saw is inherent in all organisation, now acting in the context of living systems. The English expressions 'anarchic' and 'law of the jungle' render but two facets of its sense. In fact Morin's anarchy is multifaceted: it is both the opposite of hierarchy and the generic sense of spontaneity in all living organisation. I shall congeal this flow by capitalising the greater, supra-political anarchy as Anarchy. Hierarchy, its opposite, may appear simple and inexorable but it leaks holes: it conjoins two unhomogeneous concepts each with a distinct disciplinary origin, and while Morin's method invites such conjunctions, it also seeks to avoid their simplification. One source is systems theory, the other ethology.

In systems theory hierarchy is the relationship between levels of organisation of the global system to its sub-systems. As with Jacobs' 'integron' or Koestler's 'holon', hierarchy in this sense marks the emergence of new functions. In ethology (animal studies) hierarchy concerns domination and subjugation.[38] (This is also its principal sense in political science: the two senses are much more ancient than Morin allows.)

Now even the 'integron' involves *asservissement* and with it exploitation and alienation since the sub-system is itself an individual subject, subjected to the constraints of the higher level. In this sense all life carries *asservissment*: the cell to the organ, the organ to the organism, the organism to society. But precisely because the sub-system remains an individual subject hierarchy cannot eliminate its individuality without becoming rigid and self-destructive: to be operationally effective it must respect some autonomy of the 'asservissed'. It is therefore an essential feature of all living organisation that Anarchy takes precedence over hierarchy. An organism produces itself anarchically but is organised as hierarchy.[39]

Morin dares to affirm the extreme consequence of the magnitude of disorder in the organism: 'Our body is a republic of thirty billion cells which generate hierarchies, not a hierarchy which produces a body.'[40]

The thread of Anarchy will allow us to connect the opposition of:

Acentralism–Centralism
to
Anarchy–Hierarchy

For if the body is a republic, what of its seat of government in all traditional organicism, namely the brain? For Morin the brain is the very instance which demonstrates the unbridgeable divide between the centralised command apparatus of cybernetic machines and the decentralisation of the most evolved of all brains, the human.

> The human neo-cortex is a prodigiously anarchic tissue whose synaptic lesions are randomly effected. Despite its specialised neurons its localisations occur in an undifferentiated field and can be reconstituted in other centres. The mind is precisely this active totality so that 'Mind' has no centre.[41]

There can be no foreclosure against grand Anarchy since the most complex of all organs, the brain, distinguishes itself both by its anarchy and Anarchy.

### *De-specialising the Economy*

The instance of the brain and body as confederal republics indicates why specialism is not enough. Specialisation cannot destroy the genetic capability of the individual subject to de-specialise. Morin makes enormous capital of the fact that body cells still carry the entire genetic programme of the entire body and can, sometimes, de-specialise, as can the somatically specialised insects of insect society. (So a worker bee when required becomes a queen bee.) Now, poly- and anti-specialisation are even associated with specialisation so that 'The organisation of the division of labour is always above the division of labour.'[42]

Moreover, in the long run, complexity disfavours specialisation so that human societies are likely to develop towards multi-competence. The alternative story is patently touched by faith: Morin is moved by the discoveries of biology more than by the defeats of history. When he claims that 'human societies functioned by cultural inheritance for thousands of years without a state apparatus, almost acentrically with power as a collegial, multi-headed function (assemblies of the elders)',[43] it is easy to be reminded of Kropotkin 'proving' that *Mutual Aid* was a biological rule and that government had been unknown to primitive human societies. In a canvas so wide as to include the concept of production within the control of production and of the division of labour, within the organisation of the division of labour the economic categories themselves become blurred, being bathed in the glowing colours of Anarchy. Morin's perspective is interesting: it subsumes the 'economic' under the 'cultural'. Genetically this is so since production can only take place within a culture of production; organisationally this is so since production and the division of labour can only operate if an organisation exists which makes sense of them. What is missing is the relationship in which systems of information generate specific economic structures. If indifference to the hard edges of economic categories is almost the original sin of anarchist theories, Morin's Anarchy separates him from the anarcho-Marxist rigourism of Castoriadis. So we are told that the mission of the Left is to realise 'liberal, libertarian, democratic and socialist values', but we are not told how this will happen.

When we ask what roles such a reference assigns to a market, to a command and to a communalist (or micro-social – see chapter 4) model of economic activity we can see that Morin's organisationalism has, through the concept of Anarchy as disorder, produced an implicit merger between the liberal market and libertarian communalist versions of economic modelling. In this merger there is a discrepancy between the theoretical and the emotive balance between Morin's liberalism and his libertarianism. Since the merger operated through hostility to the state, references to the functioning of the market outweigh declarations of communalist values. Thus the claim that 'The tissue of state societies, in particular their urban tissue, is constituted by spontaneous, quasi eco-organisational interactions',[44] as a validation of the market weighs more heavily than a rhetorical claim that 'we must envisage the end of class war and of economic competition.'[45]

## *The Brotherhood of Man*

As a guide for the French Left and as a use of the slender capital of 'May 1968' Morin's vision of the crisis is of great heuristic value. For the Left, Morin's myth of fraternity rescues May 1968 by transforming it retrospectively (for the Left, not Morin) into the opening drama of the crisis of hypercomplexity and thereby suppressing its original sense of a new capacity for revolutionary socialist action which for the 1968ers was an indispensable precondition for all else.

Fraternity is not the name of Morin's ultimate values, since these are humanity and love, but it is the name of their myth, since it is through fraternity that Morin organises the transition, in crisis, from the biological subject to humanity that is the entity of the fourth kind.[46] Through and in the myth Morin resolves the tension between fraternity as entry into the universal values he espouses and its cultural sediment as male bonding and armed combat. That these sediments are active in late twentieth-century French culture (in 'Morin's Ark' I referred to the widespread reproval of 'le féminisme anglo-américain') vindicates my characterisation of Morin as a Messiah-liberator 'asservissed' to the particularities of French culture. The messianic role to rescue French – and Western – culture from the dominance of centralised, patriarchal apparatuses, mobilises the resources of a French cultural archive in which fraternity as brotherhood and fraternity as humanity are fused. I argue that the 'Romulus-Remus myth' fuses two 'logics': the logic of liberation from the complex of *Oedipe* and centralised apparatus; and the logic of conservation of brotherhood.

The first 'logic' was outlined in Morin's confrontation with Lacanian psychoanalysis where he uses 'Romulus' to demonstrate that community is prior to fatherhood and the killing of Remus to show that political conflicts conjoin fraternity and fratricide. In reversing the 'psychoanalytic vulgate' Morin makes a 'mythico-real' murder the ground on which the biological Left option can expand: conflict and killing are freed from the conservative and unassuageably repetitive functions which Freud, and in his wake Lacan, had imposed. If the root of murder is patricide, which psychoanalytically denies one's own right to life, then no atonement will suffice: the 'name of the father' can be shifted – Lord, God, Master, Führer, helmsman (and why not Lacan?) – but it remains an unassuaged 'no' since human life itself (for Freud given by the father) is denied. But if the root of killing is fraternal – fratricide – the struggle can eventually be resolved since its ground is that of 'fundamentally equal egos'. A mythico-real discovery can occur: killing another, even killing the leader, is not an unatonable act since the leader is only Big Brother, he who leads in virtue of competitive pre-eminence, not out of a psychoanalytic role. The discovery is mythico-real since it combines a reversal of the Freudian myth with the profound sense of the biological discovery that *alter ego* has become *ego alter*. Fraternity can thereby operate as the psychological channel which opens entry into the entity of the fourth kind, humanity, when the human species can extend 'the humanity of love and the love of humanity'.[47]

Morin's Love is not quite consubstantial with the Freudian concept of Eros but it is palpably an enlarged version. In it the biological sources of Eros – fraternal recognition, the maternal bond, male–female sexuality – are orgasmically projected onto communication between human subjects, in which sense Morin remarks it not only expresses the highest potential of negentropy but almost removes the need for the concept of negentropy[48] since it expresses 'the reversal of dispersion'.

Nevertheless Love is 'only' the highest expression of negentropy and, as with the Freudian Eros, is fated to be locked in with its ultimately more powerful adversary, entropy-thanatos-death. In this struggle Love thus represents the final stage of Morin's Heraclitean reconciliation with death's ubiquity. Morin had reconciled himself with death intellectually, first through the concepts of entropy, of self-organisation and the complexity of genetic organisation. The *oikos*, with its exuberance of life as the economic solution to the ubiquity of death, had given him the myth of life as Osiris, to combine with intellectual acceptance of the economic 'logic' of death. Love thus crowns this acceptance, since we humans bestow it upon ourselves precisely and only because we are mortal. And mythologically through fraternity-fratricide Love can tolerate murder and can be born out of the banding of brothers. As a myth Morin's fraternity is hard to distinguish from the fraternalist mythologies in which the revolutionary France of 1789, the France of the Left, the mythological figure on the frontispiece, asserted herself as a universal and amortal feminine while nevertheless remaining rooted in the real social functions of brotherhood.

This interpretation is supported by the one instance when Morin analysed the masculine–feminine relationship, namely, his concluding article for *Femme*.[49] Here he suggested that masculine and feminine traits had biologically distinct origins but were culturally merging so that the sexual bond (Eros) could act as a major force in their continuing merger; although the language of fraternity was absent from this text, its 'logic' of the cultural transformation of an originally biological conflict was already foreshadowed.

Writing in 1971 Morin naturally responded to 'neo-feminism' in the context of all the liberationist movements of class, nationhood and age which had been promoted by May 1968. He argued against any reduction of woman to an oppressed social class and insisted on the bio-social origin and character of this 'class like no other'. This bio-social root would permit, but not ensure, the interweaving of femininity and fraternity.

Morin accorded to neo-feminism the status of a new historical actor who had arrived between 1967 and 1971, but the actor herself was an unstable interaction between her origin – femininity – and her catalyst – feminism. Femininity combined the biological functions (reproduction and nurturing) and the primate role of subordination to the male, with the historical development which by 1971 culminated in modern mass culture with woman as provider and seeker of gratification. Feminism, the adversarial politicisation of femininity, profoundly rechannelled it in posing the identity question, 'what is a woman?' And since the question addressed the most primordial of bio-social divisions, feminism opened up an interrogation into our human nature.

Feminism, however, could not answer its own questions; it was trapped between the Leftist reduction of woman to a social class and the lesbian rejection of femininity in its relationship with men. These barriers were unavoidable since the bio-social class of woman was necessarily incomplete. So without excluding the possibility of a utopian solution to these short-circuits Morin rested his principal hopes on the groundswell of radicalised femininity in an 'equilibrium where the feminine will absorb the masculine, the masculine the feminine'.[50]

In practical terms this 'osmosis' legitimated the egalitarianism of equal opportunities and the secularist libertarianism of freedom for the uterus. But it would nevertheless bond male and female in a 'Siamese universe where each is irrigated by the other's blood'.[51]

Morin's place in the extended family of the Left is thus governed by Anarchy, namely the dissociation of culture from the state and the attendant focus on the dangers of power upon the state apparatus. Anarchy is not anarchism: on the contrary, the concept of *asservissement* offers a radical exploration of the biological roots of all domination and exploitation. But the crises of *asservissement* and subjugation always arise with centralised apparatuses, especially the 'apparatus of apparatuses'. Morin does allude to the *asservissements* and subjugations of the pre-state fraternal cultures as in their 'rules for sharing women'. But his fears are focused on the dangers of state power. There seems a pervasive assumption that through Anarchy fraternal conflict can dissolve its own tendencies to *asservissement* and subjugation. Through fraternity and fratricide Morin still carries the odour of the band of brothers insurgent against 'the father', as first happened in 1789 and last in 1968 (with a phantom echo in 1995). On the French Left he is marginal and yet at home.

CHAPTER 9

# Earth Motherland

Earth, Morin declares, is our *Matrie* – motherland. So, I asked, why did you not title *terre-patrie, terre-matrie*? In French, he replied, *patrie* is grammatically feminine and conceptually masculine-feminine, a 'mère patrie, terre-mère'. But I felt unanswered since Morin demands our love for *matrie* while *patrie* 'gives paternal power to the state'.[1]

Morin's choice indicated how a fraternalist message emerges from anarchy but concludes with the unified world nation, site of love *and* power, the matrilocal *matrie* calling forth the fraternal-paternal world state.

An initial condition was required, namely the death of Stalinistic totalitarianism, an event so ardently conceived that in 1983 Morin virtually prophesied the Gorbachev revolution and Gorbachev's demise.

The anticipated human nation incorporated Morin's increasingly emotive Europeanism: the human nation would not be the opposite of Europe but its fulfilment since European culture required an idea of Europe as a unified multiplicity, an arena of cultures whose unity was constituted by their openness to all human thought.[2] Morin's analysis of Europe as a dialogic of all cultures reworked the Marxist concept upheld by 'Young Morin' of a human nature defined only by the absence of boundaries. Fulfilment, however, has itself become a darkened concept. The world nation would be marked not by the success but by the crisis of development, and be not a solution to human problems but a 'gospel of perdition'.

So in conclusion I set the grandeur of Morin's messianism against its pitfalls.

## *Morin the Prophet*

In *URSS* (*USSR*) (1983) Morin settled his account with 'apparatus communism': 'The Soviet adventure is the question of modern man, Communism that of my life.'[3]

That the book sprang from articles commissioned by Serge July,[4] editor of *Libération* and ex-1968 Leftist, speaks for Morin's agency in the twilight of Marxism in France. Morin's family quarrels with

Lefort and Castoriadis over totalitarianism now moved to the fore of French political culture.

In 1957 Lefort characterised Morin's apparatus as a 'demonology of power'. In 1983 the demon turned out to be information which *La Méthode* had made prior to production. The analysis of totalitarianism in terms of apparatus developed the emphasis on the party state Morin already held in 1957 through the concept of self-organisation.

Seen through the apparatus the attempt at total control of information carried infinite energy and infinite weakness. The attempt gave apparatus communism infinite energy; its unavoidable failure gave it infinite weakness.

The organisational logic of apparatus communism had to be understood as a strategy rather than a deducible consequence of Marxism. The strategy reclaims each event as a total confirmation for its capacity to interpret the course of history and to act upon this correct decoding of information. So to itself it always appears to march forward even when that march takes shape as a flight from the reality of events.[5]

Now not only is there a uniduality between the apparatus and the myth in whose image reality is decoded, but the myth itself is single and double since it is both a scientific claim and absolute faith in that claim.[6]

Even before it seized/created the Soviet state the Bolshevik Party was thus a dual power, being both a church militant and a civilian army and already possessed by its myth. The seizure of power generated a further duality since the Party now commanded the historic model of the command apparatus, namely the state. Each released the other's 'asservissing' capacities although ultimate control must always be lodged in 'the Party'.[7]

In political terms totalitarianism focuses on the control of control. Sociologically, the function of self-control resided in the Party, but mythologically the Party controls itself in being possessed by its science-faith, transmitted to each member in the injunction 'the Party orders you'. The apparatus cannot be lodged in institutions of state: the army and even the secret police are no more than instances of control. Conversely apparatus could develop as a special function within the Party, as happened with the secretariat presided by Stalin, and thence spread through the Party-state complex. The historic opposition between *apparatchik* and bureaucrat was therefore one of function more than institution.

The *apparatchik* both needed and fought the bureaucrat since the function (control of control) was always a mission (possession by the myth) such that the struggle against bureaucratic sclerosis was necessary to sustain the mission.[8] This struggle was generalised in the Party through the self-verificatory, inquisitorial process of the 'bio' (the autobiography demanded by the secretariat from each member).[9]

The fundamental problem of apparatus control resided in the 'bio' prior to any specific problem of management. Against commentators who suggested a collapse through economic or national difficulties Morin predicted that collapse would come from the apparatus itself.[10] The need to control and yet be possessed by its myth drove the apparatus to control information in producing pseudo and disinformation.

Ironically when Gorbachev made *glasnost* (openness) the lever which dismantled 'totalitarianism' he almost echoed Morin's claims for the primacy of information over production. Morin's claim, however, involved a perceived disjunction between the apparatus (in control of information) and a 'civil society', partly responsible for production via the black economy. Morin admitted the existence of 'civil society' (generally seen as incompatible with totalitarianism) concealed in the recesses of private life including the black economy.[11] Morin's analysis could thus admit that the totalitarian state did not exercise total control by envisaging the autonomy of social life as simply the anarchy needed by all self- re-organising beings. Official controls and myths co-existed with officially non-existent communal relationships: indeed apparatus only survived through the unacknowledged black economy. Tacitly there was collaboration, a 'social contract', since civil society was both an arena of anarchic resistance as well as the source of sustenance for apparatus.[12] What Morin's analysis excluded were the de facto institutional constraints under which the Soviet state operated and through which its economic crisis intensified. (The elimination of forced labour under Brezhnev was buttressed by automatic rights to employment guaranteed by the trade unions. In 1983 serfdom applied to South African, not Soviet, workers.) Hence Morin's analysis coarsened the dialogic into a 'duologic' (my neologism) since it left apparatus and civil society to struggle symbiotically and leave no institutional consequences. It only saved the vision of control through information by partly placing production into the anarchic black economy; but this meant that, contrary to his concept of information as a control of production, Morin partly expelled it from the sphere of production. In Morin's terminology he had failed to give full employment to the concept of information. Such under-employment is a frequent event when a concept has been stretched beyond common language use in that the user reverts to common speech in moments of crisis. The Party state presented precisely such a critical challenge to Morin as to elicit a 'Freudian slip' towards the ordinary sense of information. Glinting through Morin's analysis of the symbiotic struggle between the apparatus and civil society we can see the reality of a system where the Party state had lost total control not only over production but information. The real freedom of information in the system could have been explained in terms of the vast extent of private communication.

Ironically then, Morin's prophetic capacity may have stemmed from Gorbachev's personal commitment to information over production. Morin expected that cracks in the apparatus could come from the private lives of the *apparatchik* so that his own emphasis on the 'bio' – going back to *Autocritique* – was vindicated.

The priority Morin gave to apparatus communism also made for a family quarrel with Castoriadis. Where Castoriadis predicted that the Soviet system's thrust for global power would turn it into a 'stratocracy'[13] (a military-industrial state) Morin argued that the global ambitions were part of apparatus's flight-march forward from its internal deadlocks.[14]

The implications drawn by Morin were to give high profile to Europeanism. In the narrow sense this concerned support for the political-military version of the little Europe of its Western half but the more fundamental response had to be the extension of Europeanism using its capacity to be a universal culture to spread east even into the apparatus of the Soviet system whose military power was only a high danger because 'asservissed' to apparatus communism. What had begun in Moscow could only end in Moscow[15] (as Gorbachev would prove in 1989).

## *Strangling at Birth?*

To paraphrase Goethe: 'Beware of your prophecies because they will be fulfilled.' In *Patrie* Morin acknowledged that humanity, freed from Big Brother, was strangling at birth. To denounce the Marxist myth of salvation had served Morin as a shadow of salvation but now the false rationalities have spread all over the planet.

For a 'gospel of perdition', the salvation myths were irrecuperable; in particular the socialist adventure could not be recommenced. In *Patrie* Morin drew the consequences of biotic *asservissement* more explicitly than before: 'domination and *asservissement* are the biological roots of exploitation'.[16] Socialism could be an orientation but not a promise.

Looking at the planet in 1993 Morin saw the breakdown of self-regulatory functions everywhere. Already in 1973 Morin had asked whether the world was experiencing a crisis on the path to development or a crisis in the concept of development.[17] In 1993 he unequivocally endorsed his earlier verdict: the crisis in development derived from the inadequacy of models based on a technological-rationalist human imperialism against nature, which measured development as increments in production.

But for Morin there was supplementary bitterness since breakdowns were especially prominent in those arenas of danger where he earlier had hopes of salvation.

'Asservissed' to techno-science the information revolution had been catastrophic, incapable even of meeting techno-rationalist criteria: unlike cars, computers simply deprived humans of work.[18]

The collapse of apparatus communism transformed its flight to the future into a flight to the past. The years 1977–80 (when Marxism ceased to dominate the French intelligentsia) had been a turning point in the re-equipment not only of religious but ethno-nationalist fundamentalism.[19] Backward flight threatened to Balkanise the entire planet and so impose an ironic contradiction. The break-up of multi-national communist empire, he reiterated, had carried possibilities of renovation. But Balkanisation was nowhere worse than in Bosnia. The dissolution of a multi-ethnic cultural community would assassinate the European idea. Morin affirmed in 1992 that Bosnia had been part of a multi-ethnic Yugoslavia and so noted bitterly a regression from the liberal aspects of Yugoslavia which, in 1949, had sparked his resistance to Stalinism.[20]

## *What is to be Thought?*

Federate the earth Morin responds. It is not a realistic hope, it is the only hope. But because of his abiding faith in self-generating spontaneous process, the solution is more desperate that he appreciates. The federation he proposes requires a reform of thought which could only be the work of the European, if not French, intelligentsia. If Europe should become the world, Morin's world nation can only be a projection of Europe. Institutionally the federation should diminish, not increase, state bureaucracies. 'The UN should become a centre of decentralisation ... formulating common programmes as at Rio in 1992 ... founded on world public opinion.'[21]

Such suggestions conjoin the assumption of moral elites that being moral makes them less bureaucratic, with the belief, elsewhere criticised by Morin, that to repudiate Westernisation creates a liberating contact with all humanity. The complexity and relativism of Morin's objectives are such that only European, if not Parisian, public opinion can respond since only a thin upper crust of the world's population can afford the luxury of a world consciousness. No other public is in a position to rethink development as self-development in order to slow an unsustainable rate of change.[22]

No other public opinion can accept the mortality of cultures and yet strive to enhance cultural and regional diversity. No other public opinion could formulate the regeneration of democracy as a priority (regenerate belongs to the lexicon of 1789) in terms of the complementary antagonism of liberty, equality and fraternity.[23] In becoming more desperate the message becomes more inward-looking.

So how did Morin end with this desperate message 'unite, we are doomed'?

The voice of the 'eternal enemy' (the biological Right) will say 'Disorder has conquered: this is how the planet is and what entropy predicts. You knew it but the struggle with Big Brother left you with illusions.' But the voice of the no-less-eternal Left might say: 'You fought too hard against Big Brother; you abandoned your own double, Prometheus, the hope based on the indefeasibility of need; young Edgar Morin was right: we only appear doomed.'

If there is no voice from above Morin's method will accommodate both answers.

This most open form of Hegelianism enlisted the uncertainties of modern science precisely to meet situations where reasoning itself appears 'biodegradable'. While Morin's message seems engulfed in the terrible noise of a post-communist world his method may well prove amortal.

# Notes and References

All French publications in Paris unless otherwise stated.

## *Chapter 1*

1. H. Weinmann (ed.) *Morin: La Complexité humaine*, Flammarion, 1994.
2. For Atlan on Atlan, see 'Postulats métaphysiques et méthodes de recherche', in C. Pomiane (ed.), *La Querelle du Déterminisme*, Gallimard, 1980.
3. M. Serres, *Eclaircissements: cinq entretiens avec Bruno Latour*, Bourin, 1992.
4. T. Judt, *Marxism and the French Left*, Oxford University Press, 1986.
5. M. Poster, *Existentialist Marxism in Post-war France*, N.J., Princeton University Press, 1975.
6. For example W.H. Newton–Smith, *The Rationality of Science*, Boston, Routledge, 1981.
7. L. Althusser, *Lenin and Philosophy and other Essays,* translated by Ben Brewster, London, NLB, 1971, p. 42.
8. Morin's views in Morin, *Pour Sortir du xxème siècle*, Nathan, 1981 pp. 240–66.
9. P. Bourdieu (with L. Vacant), *Réponses (Pour une anthropologie réflexive)*, Seuil, 1992.
10. Material to 1959 based on E. Morin, *Autocritique*, Seuil, 1992.
11. See H. Weinmann in Weinmann (ed.), *Morin,* pp. 31–104 for a psychoanalytic interpretation biography in *Autocritique*.
12. E. Morin, *Vidal et les siens*, (with V. Grappe-Nahoum and H.V. Sephiha) Seuil, 1989, pp. 112–13.
13. Morin, *Autocritique,* pp. 17–21.
14. Morin's CV issued by CNRS.
15. E. Morin, 'Ce qui a changé dans la vie intellectuelle française', *Le Débat* No.40, May 1986, pp. 72–84.
16. See E. Morin *Le Vif du sujet*, Seuil, 1969.
17. C. Castoriadis, *Entretien avec Cornélius Castoriadis*, Librairie des Deux Mondes, 1975.

18. J. Robin, 'Edgar Morin et le "groupe des Dix"', in D. Bougnoux, J.L. Le Moigne, S. Proulx (eds), *Colloque de Cerisy: Arguments pour une méthode*, autour d'Edgar Morin, Seuil, 1990, pp. 82–6.
19. A. Daleux, 'L'univers selon Edgar Morin et Pierre Teilhard de Chardin', *Oméga* No.13, June 1986.
20. D. Bohm, *Wholeness and the Implicate Order*, London, Ark, 1983.
21. H. Atlan, 'Entre causalité et finalité' (debate with Morin), in Bougnoux *et al.*, *Colloque*, pp. 247–53.
22. E. Morin, *Penser l'Europe*, Gallimard, 1987, pp. 18–19.
23. Morin CV.
24. Morin, 'Vie intellectuelle', p. 78.
25. *Ibid.*, p. 72.
26. *Twentieth Century*, p. 242.
27. Morin, 'Vie intellectuelle', p. 77.
28. *Ibid.*, p. 74.
29. *Ibid.*, p. 76.
30. *Ibid.*, p. 80.
31. E. Morin, 'Messie, mais non', in Bougnoux *et al.*, *Colloque*, pp. 254–68.
32. E. Morin, *Journal de Californie*, Seuil, 1983, p. 196.
33. Morin, *Twentieth Century*, p. 251.

## *Chapter 2*

1. See Jacqueline Mer, *Le Parti de Maurice Thorez ou le bonheur communiste français: étude anthropologique*, Payot, 1977.
2. Compare to Raymond Aron, *L'Opium des Intellectuels*, Calman-Lévy, 1955.
3. Also argued by Gil Delannoi, *Crise intellectuelle et tentatives de fondation d'une politique de l'homme: 'Arguments', Edgar Morin, Jean Paul Sartre*, unpublished thesis for L'institut d'Etudes Politiques, Paris.
4. Morin, *Autocritique*, p. 42.
5. *Ibid.*, pp. 56–7.
6. *Ibid.*, p. 56.
7. *Ibid.*, p. 133.
8. M. Merleau-Ponty, *Humanisme et Terreur*, Gallimard, 1947.
9. J. Duvignaud, *Le ça perché*, Stock, 1976, p. 125.
10. Morin, *Autocritique*, pp. 98–100.
11. *Ibid.*, p. 60.
12. *Ibid.*, pp. 20–2.
13. *Ibid.*, p. 20.
14. *Ibid.*, p. 28.
15. *Ibid.*, p. 52.
16. *Ibid.*, pp. 63, 51.

17. *Ibid.*, pp. 66–8.
18. *Ibid.*, p. 68.
19. *Ibid.*, p. 62.
20. *Ibid.*, p. 86.
21. *Ibid.*, p. 86.
22. *Ibid.*, p. 86.
23. See Mer, *Le Parti de Maurice Thorez.*
24. Morin, *Autocritique*, p. 90.
25. *Ibid.*, p. 91.
26. *Ibid.*, p. 92.
27. *Ibid.*, p. 120.
28. *Ibid.*, p. 99.
29. *Ibid.*, p. 100.
30. *Ibid.*, p. 86.
31. *Ibid.*, pp. 120–2.
32. See M. Merleau-Ponty, *Les Aventures de la dialectique*, Gallimard, 1955.
33. F. Fejto, 'L'Affaire Rajk est une affaire Dreyfus internationale', *Esprit*, November 1949, pp. 690–751.
34. Morin, *Autocritique*, pp. 124–5.
35. *Ibid.*, pp. 128–31.
36. *Ibid.*, p. 104.
37. *Ibid.*, pp. 130–1.
38. Collection Jean Lacroix, *Université Catholique de Lyon,* Althusser to Lacroix, December 1949.
39. Morin, *Autocritique*, p. 153.
40. *Ibid.*, p. 153.
41. *Ibid.*, p. 152.
42. *Ibid.*, pp. 159–66.
43. *Ibid.*, p. 166.
44. *Ibid.*, p. 167.
45. *Ibid.*, pp. 167–74.
46. *Ibid.*, pp. 183–9.
47. *Ibid.*, p. 199.

## *Chapter 3*

1. G. Bataille, 'Le paradoxe de la mort et la pyramide', *Critique*, July 1953, pp. 623–1, 625.
2. E. Morin, *L'Homme et la mort,* Seuil, 1977, pp. 328–9.
3. *Ibid.*, p. 117.
4. Mascolo, *Le Communisme: Révolution et communication ou la dialetique des valeurs et des besoins*, Gallimard, 1953.
5. Morin, *L'Homme* p. 328.
6. *Ibid.*, p. 328.
7. *Ibid.*, p. 357.
8. *Ibid.*, p. 328.

9. *Ibid.*, p. 31.
10. *Ibid.*, pp. 95–119.
11. *Ibid.*, p. 27.
12. *Ibid.*, p. 33.
13. *Ibid.*, pp. 42–4.
14. *Ibid.*, p. 72.
15. *Ibid.*, p. 73.
16. *Ibid.*, p. 39.
17. *Ibid.*, pp. 228–32.
18. *Ibid.*, pp. 68.
19. *Ibid.*, pp. 72–5.
20. *Ibid.*, pp. 74–5.
21. *Ibid.*, p. 153.
22. *Ibid.*, p. 153.
23. *Ibid.*, pp. 219–26.
24. *Ibid.*, pp. 60–5.
25. *Ibid.*, pp. 287–93.
26. A. Kojève, *Introduction à la lecture de Hegel*, Gallimard, 1947.
27. *Ibid.*, pp. 288–9.
28. Morin, *L'Homme*, pp. 291–2.
29. *Ibid.*, pp. 80–1.
30. *Ibid.*, pp. 290–1.
31. *Ibid.*, p. 291.
32. *Ibid.*
33. Compare Morin, *L'Homme*, pp. 299–316 with G. Lukacs, *The Destruction of Reason*, translated by P. Palmer, London, Merlin, 1980.
34. Morin, *L'Homme*, pp. 316–19.
35. *Ibid.*, p. 276.
36. *Ibid.*, p. 324.
37. Morin, *Autocritique*, p. 187.
38. See Morin, *L'Homme*, pp. 329–45.
39. *Ibid.*, p. 330.
40. Morin, *Autocritique* p. 112.
41. Morin, *L'Homme*, p. 339.
42. Morin, *Californie*, p. 91.
43. Morin, *L'Homme*, pp. 346–7.
44. *Ibid.*, p. 349.
45. *Ibid.*, pp. 348–9.
46. *Ibid.*, p. 351.
47. *Ibid.*, p. 350.

## *Chapter 4*

1. *Arguments* No.1, January 1957, p. 1.
2. E. Morin, 'Que Faire?', *Arguments* No.16, December 1959, p. 3.

3. *Arguments* No.1, p. 1.
4. *Arguments* No.14, April 1959.
5. J. Duvignaud, 'Ce qu'il y a d'irrepréssible en l'homme', *Arguments* No.14, April 1959, pp. 4–6.
6. Morin, 'Que Faire?', p. 1.
7. K. Axelos, 'Approche du nihilisme, aphorismes systématiques', *Arguments* No.14, April 1959, pp. 2–4.
8. J. Duvignaud, 'Marxisme': idéologie ou philosophie?' *Arguments* No.2, March 1957, pp. 5–8.
9. Reprinted in E. Morin, *Introduction à une politique de l'homme, suivi d'arguments politiques*, Seuil, 1969, p. 313.
10. Morin, 'Que Faire?', p. 4.
11. *Ibid.*
12. Reprinted in Morin, *Politique*, p. 314.
13. *Ibid.*, p. 34.
14. *Ibid.*, p. 35.
15. *Ibid.*, p. 34.
16. *Arguments* No.7, May, 1958, pp. 8–13.
17. *Arguments* Nos 25–26, June 1962, pp. 2–4.
18. E. Morin, *Mes Démons*, Stock, 1994, p. 225.
19. Going back to *SB*, September 1950, No.7.
20. Morin, *Autocritique*, pp. 6–8.
21. E. Morin, 'Solecisme ou barbarie', *Arguments* No.4, June 1957, pp. 13–18.
22. *Ibid.*, pp. 16–18.
23. C. Lefort, 'Sur l'article de Morin', *Arguments* No.4, June 1957, pp. 19–21.
24. Reprinted in *Politique*, p. 316.
25. *Arguments* Nos 27–28, July 1962.
26. Morin, *Le Vif*, p. 8.
27. *Ibid.*, p. 31.
28. *Ibid.*, p. 27.
29. J. Gabel, *La fausse conscience: essai sur la réification*, Minuit, 1962.
30. Morin, *Le Vif*, p. 34.
31. Morin, *Politique*, p. 17.
32. *Ibid.*, p. 45.
33. *Ibid.*, p. 47.
34. *Ibid.*, p. 60.
35. *Ibid.*, p. 64.
36. *Ibid.*, p. 88.
37. E. Morin, *Mai '68: la brèche* (with C. Lefort and C. Castoriadis), Fayard, 1968, pp. 11–33.
38. *Ibid.*, p. 23.
39. C. Lefort, 'Le désordre nouveau', pp. 40–58; J.M. Coudray, 'La révolution anticipée', *Ibid.*, pp. 91–107.

40. A. Touraine, *Le Mouvement de Mai ou le communisme utopique*, Seuil, 1972, p. 209.
41. Morin, *Californie*, p. 7.
42. *Ibid.*, p. 117.

## *Chapter 5*

1. E. Morin, *La Nature de la nature*, Seuil, 1980, p. 124.
2. *Ibid.*, p. 30.
3. For Morin's ambiguous use of Bohm see Sean Kelly, 'Dialogue on Science, Society and the Generative Order', in *Zygon: Journal of Religion and Science*, 4 December 1990.
4. Morin, *Nature*, p. 19.
5. E. Morin, *Les idées, leur habitat, leur vie, leurs moeurs, leur organisation*, Seuil, 1991, p. 9.
6. Morin, *Nature*, p. 7.
7. *Ibid.*, p. 18.
8. E. Morin, *La Connaissance de la connaissance*, Seuil, 1986, pp. 23–4.
9. Morin, *Nature*, p. 17.
10. *Ibid.*, p. 11.
11. *Ibid.*, p. 12.
12. *Ibid.*, pp. 12–15.
13. *Ibid.*, pp. 15–24.
14. Morin, *Connaissance*, p. 98.
15. E. Morin, *Le Paradigme perdu, la nature humaine*, Seuil, 1973, pp. 98–100.
16. *Connaissance*, p. 98.
17. E. Morin, *Science avec conscience*, Fayard, 1982, pp. 145–56 for Morin's argument.
18. *Ibid.*, p. 155.
19. Morin, *Nature*, p. 15.
20. P. Feyerabend, *Against Method*, London, NLB, 1975.
21. Morin, *Connaissance*, pp. 100–1.
22. *Ibid.*, pp. 101–2.
23. *Ibid.*, pp. 102–5.
24. *Ibid.*, pp. 222–30.
25. *Ibid.*, pp. 20–2.
26. Kelly, 'Dialogue on Science'.
27. E. Morin, 'La Révolution des Savants', *Le Nouvel Observateur*, 7 December 1970.
28. *Ibid.*, p. 57.
29. Morin, *Nature*, pp. 41–2.
30. Morin, *Science*, p. 193.
31. Morin, *Nature*, p. 33.

32. *Ibid.*, p. 37.
33. Morin, *Science*, p. 33.
34. Morin, *Nature*, p. 38.
35. *Ibid.*, p. 50.
36. Morin, *Science*, p. 174.
37. *Ibid.*
38. Morin, *Nature*, pp. 86–7.
39. *Ibid.*, p. 38.
40. *Ibid.*, p. 36.
41. *Ibid.*, p. 39.
42. *Ibid.*, pp. 39–41.
43. *Ibid.*, pp. 74–8.
44. Morin, *Science*, pp. 206–11.
45. Morin, *Connaissance*, pp. 215–17.
46. Morin, *Nature*, p. 61.
47. *Ibid.*, pp. 367–8.
48. *Ibid.*, p. 75.
49. *Ibid.*, p. 57.
50. Morin, *Science*, p. 197.
51. See especially R. Thom, 'Halte au Hazard, silence au bruit', in C. Pomiane (ed.) *La Querelle du Déterminisme*, Gallimard, 1980, pp. 61–78.
52. Morin, *Démons*, p. 233.

## *Chapter 6*

1. S. Proulx, 'Paradigme Cybernétique', in *Colloque*, pp. 195–202.
2. For Marxist system theory see Y. Barel, *La réproduction sociale*, Anthropos, 1973.
3. Morin, *Nature*, pp. 157–60.
4. *Ibid.*, p. 64.
5. Morin, *Nature*, p. 78.
6. E. Morin, *La Vie de la vie*, Seuil, 1980, p. 351 and passim.
7. *Ibid.*, pp. 274–5.
8. Morin, *Nature*, p. 207.
9. Morin, *Vie*, p. 171.
10. *Ibid.*, p. 440.
11. *Ibid.*, p. 284.
12. *Ibid.*, pp. 171–2.
13. *Ibid.*, p. 185.
14. J. Derrida, *L'écriture et la différence*, Seuil, 1967, pp. 70–90.
15. Morin, *Vie*, pp. 177–83.
16. *Ibid.*, pp. 178–9.
17. *Ibid.*, p. 181.
18. *Ibid.*, p. 187.

19. *Ibid.*, p. 188.
20. *Ibid.*, p. 271.
21. *Ibid.*, p. 271.
22. *Ibid.*, p. 272.
23. *Ibid.*, pp. 333–46.
24. Morin, *Nature*, p. 94.
25. *Ibid.*, pp. 98–103.
26. *Ibid.*, pp. 97–103.
27. *Ibid.*, p. 100.
28. *Ibid.*, p. 142.
29. *Ibid.*, p. 125.
30. *Ibid.*, pp. 103–4.
31. *Ibid.*, pp. 112, 134.
32. *Ibid.*, p. 106.
33. *Ibid.*, p. 112.
34. *Ibid.*, p. 147.
35. *Ibid.*, p. 122.
36. *Ibid.*, p. 123.
37. *Ibid.*, p. 174.
38. *Ibid.*, p. 157.
39. *Ibid.*, p. 165.
40. *Ibid.*, p. 174.
41. *Ibid.*, p. 184.
42. Morin, *Vie*, p. 131.
43. Morin, *Nature*, p. 206.
44. *Ibid.*, p. 239.
45. *Ibid.*, pp. 291–6.
46. *Ibid.*, p. 300.
47. *Ibid.*, p. 297.
48. *Ibid.*, p. 298.
49. *Ibid.*, p. 239.
50. *Ibid.*, p. 254.
51. *Ibid.*, pp. 317–18.
52. *Ibid.*, p. 256.
53. *Ibid.*, pp. 239–47.
54. *Ibid.*, p. 246.
55. *Ibid.*, p. 243.
56. *Ibid.*, p. 253.
57. *Ibid.*, p. 253.

## *Chapter 7*

1. Morin, *Connaissance*, p. 114.
2. *Ibid.*, p. 111.
3. *Ibid.*, p. 97.

4. *Ibid.*, p. 76.
5. *Ibid.*, pp. 83, 84.
6. *Ibid.*, p. 82.
7. *Ibid.*, pp. 72–3.
8. *Ibid.*, pp. 111–13.
9. *Ibid.*, p. 109.
10. *Ibid.*, p. 172.
11. *Ibid.*, pp. 139–42.
12. *Ibid.*, p. 142.
13. *Ibid.*, p. 154.
14. *Ibid.*, pp. 156–58.
15. *Ibid.*, p. 82.
16. Morin, *Idées*, p. 111.
17. *Ibid.*, p. 122.
18. *Ibid.*, p. 165.
19. Morin, *Connaissance*, p. 171.
20. Morin, *Idées*, pp. 178–79.
21. *Ibid.*, pp. 184–5.
22. *Ibid.*, p. 197.
23. *Ibid.*, p. 194.
24. *Ibid.*, p. 196.

## *Chapter 8*

1. G. Busino (ed.) 'Radioscopie d'Edgar Morin', *Revue Européenne des Sciences Sociales*, Geneva, Vol. 25, No.75, 1987.
2. Morin, *Vie*, p. 328.
3. *Ibid.*, p. 248.
4. *Ibid.*, p. 328.
5. *Ibid.*, p. 436.
6. E. Morin, *Le rose et le noir*, Galilée, 1984.
7. Morin, *Vie*, p. 436.
8. This concept had already emerged in 1976. See E. Morin, *Sociologie*, Fayard, 1994, pp. 175–90.
9. Morin, *Vie*, pp. 326–7.
10. See E. Morin, *Terre-Patrie* (with A.B. Kern), Seuil, 1993 p. 161.
11. Morin, *Vie*, p. 431.
12. *Ibid.*, p. 428.
13. *Ibid.*, p. 430.
14. *Ibid.*, p. 417.
15. *Ibid.*, pp. 237–9.
16. *Ibid.*, p. 31.
17. *Ibid.*, p. 32.
18. *Ibid.*, pp. 47–69.

19. Morin, *Nature*, p. 347.
20. Morin, *Paradigm Lost*, pp. 63–82.
21. Morin, *Vie*, p. 245.
22. Morin, *Paradigm Lost*, p. 58.
23. Morin, *Vie*, p. 245.
24. *Ibid.*, pp. 439–42.
25. *Ibid.*, p. 439.
26. *Ibid.*, p. 440.
27. *Ibid.*, p. 440.
28. *Ibid.*, p. 440.
29. C. Castoriadis, *L'Institution imaginaire de la société*, Seuil, 1975.
30. *Ibid.*, p. 247.
31. *Ibid.*, p. 248.
32. *Ibid.*, pp. 248, 251; see *Patrie*.
33. Morin, *Vie*, p. 249.
34. *Ibid.*, p. 250.
35. *Ibid.*, pp. 250–1.
36. My grid is based on Morin, *Vie*, pp. 305, 309, 315.
37. Morin, *Vie*, p. 322.
38. *Ibid.*, pp. 309–10.
39. *Ibid.*, p. 314.
40. *Ibid.*, p. 310.
41. *Ibid.*, p. 318.
42. *Ibid.*, p. 308.
43. *Ibid.*, p. 317.
44. *Ibid.*, p. 317.
45. *Ibid.*, p. 328.
46. *Ibid.*, p. 447.
47. *Ibid.*, p. 443.
48. *Ibid.*, p. 443.
49. E. Morin, *La femme majeure, nouvelle féminité, nouveau féminisme* (with N. Benoît and B. Paillard), Seuil, 1973, pp. 131–53.
50. *Ibid.*, p. 153.
51. *Ibid.*, p. 142.

## *Chapter 9*

1. Morin, *Patrie*, p. 81.
2. Morin, *Europe*, pp. 234–6.
3. E. Morin, *De la nature de l'URSS*, Fayard, 1983, p. 9.
4. *URSS*, p. 10.
5. *URSS*, pp. 40–2.
6. *URSS*, p. 50.
7. *URSS*, p. 59.
8. *URSS*, p. 76–8.

9. *URSS*, p. 133.
10. *URSS*, pp. 225–39.
11. *URSS*, pp. 146–9.
12. *URSS*, p. 153.
13. C. Castoriadis, *Devant la Guerre*, Fayard, 1980.
14. *URSS*, pp. 198–214.
15. *URSS*, pp. 238–54.
16. Morin, *Patrie*, p. 121.
17. Morin, *Sociologie*, pp. 444–7.
18. Morin, *Patrie*, p. 75.
19. *Ibid.*, p. 99.
20. H. Weinmann (ed.), *Morin*: 1994, p. 244.
21. Morin, *Patrie*, pp. 137–8.
22. *Ibid.*, pp. 89–95.
23. Morin, *Patrie*, p. 170.

# Bibliography

## *Morin's Works (thematically arranged with short titles)*

All French publications in Paris unless otherwise stated.


### *La Méthode*

*La Nature de la nature* (Vol. I), Seuil, 1980. (*Nature*)
*La Vie de la vie* (Vol. II), Seuil, 1980. (*Vie*)
*La Connaissance de la connaissance* (Vol. III), Seuil, 1986. (*Connaissance*)
*Les idées, leur habitat, leur vie, leurs moeurs, leur organisation* (Vol. IV), Seuil, 1991. (*Idées*)

### *Complex Thought*

*Science avec conscience*, Fayard, 1982. (*Science*)
*Science et conscience de la complexité* (presented by C. Attais and J.L. Le Moigne), Université, Aix-en-Provence, 1984.
*Sociologie*, Fayard, 1994.
*Introduction à la pensée complexe*, ESF, 1990.

### *Human Sciences*

*L'Homme et la mort*, Seuil, 1977. (*L'Homme*)
*Le Cinéma ou l'homme imaginaire*, Minuit, 1956. (*Cinéma*)
*Le Paradigme perdu, la nature humaine*, Seuil, 1973. (*Paradigm Lost*)
*L'Unité de l'homme* (with M. Piatelli-Palmarini), Seuil, 1974.

### *Twentieth Century*

*L'An zéro de L'Allemagne*, La Cité Universelle, 1946.
*Les Stars*, Seuil, 1957.
*L'Esprit du temps*, Grasset (Vol. 1) 1962; (Vol. 2) 1976. (*Present Time*)
*Commune en France: la métamorphose de Plozevet*, Fayard, 1967, translated: S. Smith, London, Allen Lane, 1971. (*Report from a French Village*)

*Mai '68: la brèche* (with C. Lefort and C. Castoriadis), Fayard, 1968. (*Mai '68*)

*La Rumeur d'Orléans*, Seuil, 1969, translated: P. Green, London, Blond, 1971. (*Rumour in Orleans*)

*La femme majeure, nouvelle féminité, nouveau féminisme* (with N. Benoît and B. Paillard), Seuil, 1973. (*Femme*)

*Pour sortir du xxème siècle*, Nathan, 1981. (*Twentieth Century*)

*De la nature de l'URSS*, Fayard, 1983. (URSS)

*Le rose et le noir*, Galilée, 1984. (*Rose*)

*Penser l'Europe*, Gallimard, 1987. (*Europe*)

*Un nouveau commencement* (with G. Bocchi and M. Ceruti), Seuil, 1991.

*Terre-Patrie* (with A.B. Kern), Seuil, 1993. (*Patrie*)

*Politics*

*Introduction à une politique de l'homme, suivi d'arguments politiques*, Seuil, 1969. (*Politique*)

*Autobiography*

*Autocritique*, Seuil, 1992.

*Le Vif du sujet*, Seuil, 1969. (*Le Vif*)

*Journal de Californie*, Seuil, 1983. (*Californie*)

*Journal d'un livre*, Inter-Editions, 1981.

*Vidal et les siens* (with V. Grappe-Nahoum and H.V. Sephiha), Seuil, 1989. (*Vidal*)

*Mes Démons*, Stock, 1994.

*Une Année de Sisyphe*, Seuil, 1995.

*Colloquia*

D. Bougnoux, J.L. Le Moigne, S. Proulx (eds), *Colloque de Cerisy: Arguments pour une méthode, autour d'Edgar Morin*, Seuil, 1990.

## *Arguments: Articles Cited*

K. Axelos, 'Approche du nihilisme, aphorismes systématiques', No. 14, April 1959.

——, 'Le jeu de L'autocritique', Nos 27–28, July 1962.

J. Duvignaud, 'Marxisme: idéologie ou philosophie?', No. 2, March 1957.

——, 'Ce qu'il y a d'irrepréssible en l'homme', No.14, April 1959.

G. Lapassade (with Morin), 'La Question micro-sociale', Nos 25–26, January 1962.

C. Lefort, 'Sur l'article de Morin', No.4, June 1957.

Morin, 'L'au delà philosophique de Marx', No.21, June 1957.
——, 'La Fin d'un commençement', Nos 27–28, July 1962.
——, 'Que Faire?', No.16, October 1959.
——, 'Questionnaire sur la pensée anticipatrice: Réponse d'Edgar Morin', No.9, September 1958.
——, 'Le révisonnisme géneralisé', No.14, April–June 1959.
——, 'Revisons le révisionisme', No.2, February–March 1957.
——, 'Solecisme ou barbarie', No.4, June 1957.

## *Other Journals and Writings*

Morin, 'Ce qui a changé dans la vie intellectuelle française', *Le Débat* No.40, May 1986.
——, 'La Révolution des Savants', *Le Nouvel Observateur*, 7 December 1970.
L. Atlar, 'Entre causalité et finalité' (debate with Morin) in *Colloque.*
G. Bataille, 'Le paradoxe de la mort et la pyramide', *Critique*, July 1953.
G. Busino (ed.), 'Radioscopie d'Edgar Morin', *Revue Européenne des Sciences Sociales,* Geneva, Vol.25, No.75, 1987.
*Collection Jean Lacroix*, Université Catholique de Lyon.
A. Daleux, 'L'Univers selon Edgar Morin et Pierre Teilhard de Chardin', *Oméga*, No.13, June 1986.
G. Delannoi, *Crise intellectuelle et tentatives de fondation d'une politique de l'homme: 'Arguments', Edgar Morin, Jean Paul Sartre*, unpublished thesis for L'institut d'Études politiques, Paris.
F. Fejto, 'L'Affaire Rajk est une affaire Dreyfus internationale', *Esprit,* November 1949.
D. Gascoyne, 'Thoughts of Edgar Morin', *Resurgence*, No.113, November 1985.
S. Kelly, 'Dialogue on Science, Society and the Generative Order', *Zygon: Journal of Religion and Science*, 4 December 1990.
——, 'Hegel and Morin: the science of wisdom and the wisdom of the new science', *The Owl of Minerva*, 20 (1): 1988.
S. Proulx, 'Paradigme Cybernétique', *Colloque*, 1990.
J. Robin, 'Edgar Morin et le "groupe des Dix"', *Colloque*, 1990.

## *Other Books Cited*

L. Althusser, *Lenin and Philosophy and other essays* (translation Ben Brewster), London, NLB, 1971.
R. Aron, *L'Opium des Intellectuels*, Calman–Levy, 1955.
H. Atlan, *Entre le crystal et la fumée; Essai sur l'organisation du vivant,* Seuil, 1979.
——, 'Postulats Métaphysiques et Méthodes de Recherche', in *La Querelle du Déterminisme*, Gallimard, 1980.

Y. Barel, *La réproduction sociale*, Anthropos, 1973.
D. Bohm, *Wholeness and the Implicate Order*, London, Ark, 1983.
P. Bourdieu (with L. Vacant), *Réponses (Pour une anthropologie réflexive)*, Seuil, 1992.
C. Castoriadis, 'La Révolution Anticipée', in *Mai '68.*
——, *Entretien avec Cornélius Castoriadis,* Libraire de Deux Mondes, 1975.
——, *L'Institution imaginaire de la Société*, Seuil, 1975.
*Devant la guerre*, Fayard 1980 is the last cited work for Castoriadis.
J. Derrida, *L'écriture et la différence*, Seuil, 1967.
J. Duvignaud, *Le ça perché*, Stock, 1976.
P. Feyerabend, *Against Method*, London, NLB, 1975.
J. Gabel, *La fausse conscience: essai sur la réification*, Minuit, 1962.
F. Jacob, *La logique du vivant: Une histoire de l'hérédité*, Gallimard, 1970.
T. Judt, *Marxism and the French Left*, Oxford, Oxford University Press, 1986.
——, *Devant la guerre*, Fayard, 1980.
A. Kojève, *Introduction à la lecture de Hegel*, Gallimard, 1947.
C. Lefort, *'Le Désordre Nouveau'*, in *Mai '68.*
G. Lukacs, *The Destruction of Reason*, translated P. Palmer, London, Merlin, 1980.
D. Mascolo, *Le Communisme: Révolution et communication ou la dialectique des valeurs et des besoins*, Gallimard, 1953.
J. Mer, *Le Parti de Maurice Thorez ou le bonheur communiste français: étude anthropologique*, Payot 1977.
M. Merleau-Ponty, *Humanisme et Terreur (Essai sur le problème communiste)*, Gallimard, 1947.
——, *Les Aventures de la dialectique*, Gallimard, 1955.
J. Monod, *Le hazard et la nécessité: essai sur la philosophie naturelle de la biologie moderne*, Seuil, 1970.
W.H. Newton-Smith, *The Rationality of Science*, Boston, Routledge, 1981.
I. Prigogine, and I. Stengers, *La Nouvelle Alliance: Métamorphose de la Science*, Gallimard, 1979.
K. Popper, *The Logic of Scientific Discovery*, London, Hutchinson, 1968.
M. Serres, *Eclaircissements: cinq entretiens avec Bruno Latour*, Bourin, 1992.
R. Thom, 'Halte au Hazard, silence au bruit', in *La Querelle du Déterminisme*, Gallimard, 1980.
A. Touraine, *Le Mouvement de Mai ou le communisme utopique*, Seuil, 1972.
H. Weinmann (ed.), *Morin: La Complexité humaine*, Flammarion, 1994.

# Index